Prominent Women OF THE 20th Century

Prominent Women OF THE 20th Century

VOLUME 1:
A-C

Edited by Peggy Saari

U·X·L

An imprint of Gale Research,
an International Thompson Publishing Company

I T P
Changing the Way the World Learns

NEW YORK • LONDON • BONN • BOSTON • DETROIT
MADRID • MELBOURNE • MEXICO CITY • PARIS
SINGAPORE • TOKYO • TORONTO • WASHINGTON
ALBANY NY • BELMONT CA • CINCINNATI OH

Prominent Women of the 20th Century

Peggy Saari, Editor

Staff

Kathleen L. Witman, *U·X·L Associate Developmental Editor*
Julie L. Carnagie, *U·X·L Assistant Developmental Editor*
Carol DeKane Nagel, *U·X·L Developmental Editor*
Thomas L. Romig, *U·X·L Publisher*

Margaret A. Chamberlain, *Permissions Specialist (Pictures)*

Shanna P. Heilveil, *Production Assistant*
Evi Seoud, *Assistant Production Manager*
Mary Beth Trimper, *Production Director*

Pamela A. E. Galbreath, *Art Director*
Cynthia Baldwin, *Product Design Manager*

Linda Mahoney, *Typesetting*

Library of Congress Cataloging-in-Publication Data

Saari, Peggy
   Prominent women of the 20th century / Peggy Saari.
      p.   cm.
   Includes bibliographical references and index.
   ISBN 0-7876-0646-4 (set). – ISBN 0-7876-0647-2 (v. 1)
   ISBN 0-7876-0648-0 (v. 2) – ISBN 0-7876-0649-9 (v. 3)
      ISBN 0-7876-0650-4 (v. 4)

   1. Women–Biography–Dictionaries. 2. Biography–20th century–
Dictionaries. I. Title. 3. Women authors–Biography–Dict.
CT3235.S2 1996
920.72'09'04 – dc20 4. Actresses   – " "   95-41363
[B] PRO   5. Singers – " "   CIP
      6. Biography

This publication is a creative work fully protected by all applicable copyright laws, as well as by misappropriation, trade secret, unfair competition, and other applicable laws. The editors of this work have added value to the underlying factual material herein through one or more of the following: unique and original selection, coordination, expression, arrangement, and classification of the information. All rights to this publication will be vigorously defended.

Printed in the United States of America

I(T)P™ U·X·L is an imprint of Gale Research Inc.,
        an International Thomson Publishing Company.
        ITP logo is a trademark under license

Contents

Maya Lin

Volume 1: A–C

Volume 2: D–I

Volume 3: J–O

Volume 4: P–Z

Fields of Endeavor

Bold numerals indicate volume numbers.

Maria Tallchief

Military

Music

Photography

Politics and Government, U.S.

Science and Medicine

Social Issues

Sports

Technology

Theater

Writing

Nationality/ Ethnicity

Bold numerals indicate volume numbers.

Women are listed by country of origin and/or citizenship as well as by ethnicity (see African American, Asian American, Hispanic American, Native American).

Benazir Bhutto

American

Rosa Parks

P rominent Women of the 20th Century presents the biographies of women whose achievements have made a significant and lasting impact on life in the twentieth century. The 200 women included in these four volumes are from a variety of ethnic backgrounds and reflect accomplishments in many fields of endeavor, including the sciences, politics and government, social activism, sports, and the arts. A number of the people featured here, such as civil rights activist Coretta Scott King, Catholic missionary Mother Teresa, and singer Gloria Estefan, may be readily recognizable to readers. Perhaps less familiar are figures such as Rosalind Franklin, the codiscoverer of the structure of DNA, or Annie Dodge Wauneka, the tribal leader who eradicated tuberculosis among the Navajo. The purpose of *Prominent Women* is both to retell the stories of extraordinary women who have inspired people throughout the world and to describe the contributions of equally remarkable women who have remained relatively unknown.

Inclusion Criteria

Individuals chosen for inclusion in *Prominent Women* fit into one or more of the following categories:

- Those who have significantly affected the course of their nation or the world, bringing about permanent or long-term change–renowned women like Eleanor Roosevelt, the U.S. first lady who advanced the cause of human rights throughout the world, and Marie Curie, the Polish-born nuclear physicist who conducted groundbreaking research in radioactivity.

- Those who have struggled against the forced limitations of gender, race, or personal circumstances to achieve their goals–courageous women such as Marie Montessori, the Italian educator who fought sexism in the medical profession; Michiko Nishiura Weglyn, the Japanese-American author who was held in "American concentration camps" during World War II; and Oksana Baiul, the Ukrainian figure skater who was orphaned at the age of 13 and went on to win an Olympic gold medal.

- Those who have made important discoveries or introduced new ideas–innovators like Susan Bell Burnell, the Irish astronomer who discovered pulsars; Madame C. J. Walker, the African American entrepreneur who developed cosmetics for black women; and Alice Evans, the American microbiologist who successfully campaigned for the pasteurization of milk.

- Those who have made important achievements in their fields of endeavor–pioneering figures such as Jacqueline Cochran, the American aviator who was the first woman to break the sound barrier; Margaret Thatcher, who became the first woman prime minister of Britain; and Judit Polgar, the Hungarian chess player who became a grand master at age 16.

Format

Each volume of *Prominent Women* begins with an alphabetical table of contents followed by two additional listings of the profilees, one organized by nationality/ethnicity and one according to field of endeavor. The entries are arranged alphabetically in four volumes. Each five- to eight-page profile opens with a portrait, birth and death information, and a quote by or about the woman. The biographies focus on early childhood and formative years, presenting the key factors involved in each woman's achievement–personal motivation or the obstacles confronted–and go on to discuss the impact of her accomplishment. Supplementing the profiles are additional photos and sidebars that highlight related events, movements, and people. Thirteen entries feature brief biographical sketches, some with accompanying portraits, of other women who made contributions in the same field. A glossary of terms is included in entries about women who have made scientific or technological achievements. A list of works for further reading is provided at the end of each profile. The volumes conclude with a cumulative subject index that provides easy access to people, movements, and works mentioned throughout *Prominent Women of the 20th Century*.

Acknowledgments

Special thanks are due for the invaluable comments and suggestions provided by U•X•L's women's books advisers:

Annette Haley, High School Librarian/Media Specialist at Grosse Ile High School in Grosse Ile, Michigan; Mary Ruthsdotter, Projects Director of the National Women's History Project; Francine Stampnitzky, Children's/Young Adult Librarian at the Elmont Public Library in Elmont, New York; and Ruth Ann Karlin Yeske, Librarian at North Middle School in Rapid City, South Dakota.

Special thanks also go to the following individuals who helped research and write many of the entries: Jon Saari, Ingrid Morgan, Rachel Moulton, Aaron Saari, and Stephen Allison.

Comments and Suggestions

We welcome your comments on this work as well as your suggestions for individuals to be featured in future editions of *Prominent Women of the 20th Century*. Please write: Editor, *Prominent Women of the 20th Century*, U•X•L, 835 Penobscot Bldg., Detroit, Michigan 48226-4094; call toll-free: 1-800-877-4253; or fax: 313-961-6348.

Photo Credits

Rita Moreno

Cover photos:

AP/Wide World Photos: Maya Angelou (top) and Madonna (bottom); **Courtesy of the Consulate General of India:** Indira Gandhi (left).

Photographs and illustrations appearing in *Prominent Women of the 20th Century* were received from the following sources:

AP/Wide World Photos: volume 1: pp. 1, 12, 23, 28, 32, 35, 38, 48, 50, 53, 54, 57, 59, 70, 80, 82, 88, 94, 96, 100, 106, 109, 111, 113, 118, 128, 130, 133, 137, 144, 146, 149, 151, 159, 164, 166, 175, 178, 181, 189, 193, 200, 212, 223, 227, 236, 238, 241, 246, 249, 256; volume 2: pp. 287, 294, 301, 303, 312, 317, 319, 326, 329, 336, 339, 342, 345, 356, 361, 364, 366, 370, 376, 388, 397, 405, 415, 421, 425, 431, 433, 436, 439, 442, 444, 446, 452, 463, 470, 474, 480, 490, 497, 501, 503, 506, 517; volume 3: pp. 539, 541, 547, 552, 555, 561, 565, 568, 576, 580, 586, 588, 590, 595, 597, 602, 607, 616, 625, 628, 629, 633, 638, 640, 646, 648, 650, 653, 659, 668, 671, 673, 680, 682, 691, 696, 698, 703, 705, 713, 716, 721, 724, 726, 729, 731, 733, 735, 738, 740, 742, 748, 750, 752, 768; volume 4: pp. 793, 796, 798, 802, 810, 813, 816, 819, 820, 823, 824, 826, 832, 835, 837, 840, 844, 853, 868, 871, 882, 889, 892, 898, 902, 905, 912, 919, 921, 928, 930, 934, 939, 943, 950, 954, 955, 963, 972, 989, 999, 1003, 1005, 1008, 1010, 1015. **Archive Photos:** volume 1: p. 229; volume 2: pp. 275, 306, 443; volume 4: p. 864. **Archive Photos/R.**

Bella Abzug

Born July 24, 1920
New York, New York

American lawyer, politician

*First Jewish U.S. congresswoman
and co-founder of the National
Women's Political Caucus*

B ella Abzug was elected to the U.S. House of Representatives after a long career as a labor lawyer, civil-liberties advocate, and peace activist. During the time she served in Congress she challenged congressional decorum by bluntly denouncing her male colleagues as a privileged elite of white, middle-aged men who were out of touch with the needs and aspirations of most Americans. Abzug was among the most vocal members of congress demanding an immediate withdrawal of American military forces from Indochina during the Vietnam conflict in the 1970s. She also took strong positions in favor of women's and minority rights and federal aid to cities.

Abzug was born Bella Savitsky on July 24, 1920, the daughter of Emanuel and Esther Savitsky. Her father was a butcher in New York City. In 1942 she graduated from Hunter College in New York with a bachelor of arts degree. Two years later she married Maurice Abzug, a stockbroker and novelist, with whom she had two daughters. After earning a

"Women have been trained to speak softly and carry a lipstick. Those days are over."

law degree from Columbia University in New York in 1947, she practiced law privately for 23 years, until she was elected to the U.S. House of Representatives.

Flamboyant congresswoman

During her two terms in Congress (1970-74) Abzug served on the committee on public works and transportation and was chair of the subcommittee on government information and individual rights. She was also assistant Democratic whip to Speaker Thomas P. O'Neill, Jr. Soon after Abzug reached the floor of Congress she became a highly visible, flamboyant figure, with her trademark wide-brimmed hats and feisty manner. While her strongly worded, forthright speeches had great popular appeal, her political allies often believed her personal style detracted from their cause. Abzug was criticized for preferring to make headlines on her own instead of negotiating and compromising to pass legislation. But the New York Democrat earned increasing respect from her colleagues over the years while remaining true to her political vision.

In her capacity as chair of the House subcommittee on government information and individual rights, Abzug conducted inquiries on covert and illegal activities by agencies of the federal government. She helped produce the "Government in the Sunshine" law, which gave the public greater access to government records. Abzug co-founded the National Women's Political Caucus in 1971 and authored numerous bills intended to prevent sex discrimination and improve the status of women. On local issues she devoted much of her time to securing federal funds for New York City during the city's fiscal crisis in the mid-1970s. In 1972 she wrote *Bella! Ms. Abzug Goes to Washington,* an account of her experiences as a congresswoman.

Returns to law practice

Abzug gave up her congressional seat in 1976 to seek the New York Democratic party nomination for the U.S. Senate, narrowly losing the race to Daniel Patrick Moynihan. She went on to run unsuccessfully for mayor of New York City in 1977 and for a congressional seat representing the East Side of Manhattan in 1978. Political analysts attributed these losses to her confrontational image and the conservative nature of the electorate. President Jimmy Carter appointed Abzug co-chair of the National Advisory Committee for Women. Carter dismissed her in 1979 after the committee issued a report criticizing the president's decision to cut funding for women's programs. She then returned to her legal practice. Abzug remained in the public eye, however, as a lecturer, television news commentator, and magazine columnist. She was also an executive for women's organizations, including Women-USA, a grass-roots political action organization, and the Women's Foreign Policy Council.

Writes book on "gender gap"

Abzug drew on her decades-long leadership experience in the women's movement to write *Gender Gap: Abzug's Guide to Political Power for Women,* which was published in 1984. With co-author Mim Kelber, Abzug examined the possible causes and political consequences of the "gender gap," the wide disparity in voting patterns between men and women noticed in some American elections. In the 1980 presidential election, for instance, many more women than men voted to reelect Carter, and the gender gap made the difference in a number of elections for state governors later in the decade. Although statisticians have had trouble identifying the specific political differences that may separate the sexes at the ballot box, Abzug credits the feminist movement for encouraging women's independence.

Becomes environmental advocate

In *Gender Gap* Abzug also outlined a range of political, social, and economic issues on which women can have an impact. Among them is the environment, an area in which Abzug herself became active in the early 1990s. Appointed as special adviser to the Secretary-General of the United Nations

Conference on Environment and Development (UNCED), she became a leading advocate of environmental security and a more economically fair world. In 1991 she was an organizer of the Women's Congress for a Healthy Planet as part of the Earth Summit sponsored by the United Nations in Rio de Janeiro, Brazil. The congress issued the "Action Agenda for the Twenty-first Century," which challenged men and women to work together for a "safe and sustainable future." Abzug identified a particular role–and a higher degree of freedom–for women in cleaning up "the mess" that has been made throughout the world: "I believe women will bring a new vision, with new perspectives as to how and what to change," she told an interviewer. "It's easier with women because they are not part of what has taken place. They aren't totally unshackled, not only by lack of ownership but by lack of involvement in decisions to date. They are freer and more independent."

Where to learn more

Abzug, Bella, *Bella! Ms. Abzug Goes to Washington,* Saturday Review Press, 1972.

Abzug, Bella (with Mim Kelber), *Gender Gap: Bella Abzug's Guide to Political Power for American Women,* Houghton, 1984.

"Bella Abzug: Giving Women a Voice," *Environmental Action,* Summer 1992, pp. 12-13.

Faber, Doris, *Bella Abzug,* Lothrop, 1976.

Joy Adamson

Born January 20, 1910
Troppau, Silesia
Died January 3, 1980
Nairobi, Kenya
Austrian naturalist

Joy Adamson gained global acclaim in the 1960s for her book *Born Free,* which led to a film and television series of the same name. In an interview Adamson observed that the enormous success of *Born Free* "proves the hunger of people to return ... to a world of genuine proportion, a world in which our balance and basic values have not been destroyed. All this shows how important it is to preserve the animal life we have left." As both naturalist and artist Adamson produced approximately 400 paintings of wildflowers, 80 drawings of coral fish, and 570 studies of African tribes. She received the Gold Grenfall Medal of the Royal Horticultural Society in 1947 for illustrating seven books on the plant life of East Africa.

Christened Friederike Viktoria Gessner, Adamson was born on January 20, 1910, in Troppau, Silesia (now Opava in the Czech Republic). Her parents were Viktor Gessner, an architect, urban planner, and civil servant, and Traute (Greipel) Gessner, whose family were wealthy paper manufacturers. After her parents divorced when she was 12 years

"Elsa opened, for me, so many completely new and staggering insights into animal psychology."

old, Adamson went to schools in Vienna, Austria. She studied music, metalworking, wood sculpting, art history, dressmaking, and design before preparing for a medical career. In 1935 she married Viktor von Klarwill, an Austrian businessman.

Immigrates to Africa

In 1937 Adamson traveled to Kenya to explore the prospect of establishing residence in East Africa. After her marriage to von Klarwill ended in divorce, she remained in Africa. In 1938 she married Peter Bally, a botanist with the Nairobi Museum. She had met Bally on the voyage to Africa, and he renamed her Joy. The couple spent their honeymoon on a scientific expedition to the Chyullu mountains, on the border of Kenya and Tanzania. A meticulous painter of flowers himself, Bally encouraged Adamson to paint the plants he collected. Adamson gradually expanded her range of subjects to include tribal life, providing valuable records for anthropologists (scientists who study human social and behavioral patterns). She also painted landscapes and animals. Adamson divorced Bally in 1942, and the following year she married George Adamson, a warden with Kenya's Game Department. Joy Adamson continued painting and contributed botanical samples to the Royal Botanical Gardens, better known as Kew Gardens, near London, England.

In 1956 George Adamson shot a lioness that attacked him when he accidentally approached her cubs. He brought the three cubs home to Adamson, who had already raised many animals. However, the chief game warden believed the cubs would be too hard to take care of. Against Adamson's wishes, he sent two of them to the city zoo in Rotterdam, Netherlands, leaving only the smallest cub, a lioness named Elsa. Losing Elsa's siblings led Adamson to open a national animal clinic and orphanage, which still operates in Nairobi more than fifty years later.

Befriends Elsa the lion cub

With Elsa, Joy Adamson commented later that she developed an "utterly genuine and simple and natural" relationship.

She claimed Elsa "could understand my thoughts and act according to them.... I know that she was not merely responding [to] my mood or from physical signals." From the outset Adamson was determined not to turn Elsa into a pet, however, and she accepted an offer from the warden of the Maasai Mara Reserve to provide Elsa with a permanent home.

The attempt failed because the cub could not adapt to her new home. Born in the high altitudes and dry climate of northern Kenya, Elsa fell ill in the hotter, more humid conditions 350 miles to the south. Moreover, George Adamson could find no way to persuade a local pride (a company of lions) to accept her.

Tells story of cubs

The district commissioner at Meru in Northern Tanzania, close to where Elsa was born, offered to let the lion live on his nature preserve. At two and a half years, Elsa was old enough to fend for herself, join a pride, and find a mate, but her upbringing had not given her the necessary skills. George Adamson helped provide her with training and looked for ways to integrate her with local prides. When it was clear that Elsa had mated, the Adamsons left her on her own. After the birth of her cubs, Elsa disappeared for six weeks, then she paid the Adamsons the first of many visits with her cubs. When Elsa was five, she died of a tick infection, and a local lioness drove the cubs out of the territory. After a long search, George Adamson found the cubs and took them to the Serengeti National Park, where they were set free. Adamson told the cubs' story in her books *Living Free* and *Forever Free,* which both became best-sellers. The film *Forever Free,* based on Adamson's books, was released in 1971.

Establishes wildlife preservation fund

Adamson's books, films, and lectures gave people a new awareness of the relations between man and animal. Because of increasing interest in wildlife, Adamson established the Elsa Wild Animal Appeal in the United Kingdom in 1961, in the United States in 1969, and in Canada in 1971. In addition to donating most of the proceeds from her books and films to this fund, she became a pioneer in efforts to protect endangered species by boycotting products made from fur and other animal parts. Increasingly preferring wild animals to people, Adamson began living by herself in 1971 at a lakeside estate outside of Nairobi. During these years she succeeded in raising a cheetah named Pippa and wrote two books about the animal, *The Spotted Sphinx* and *Pippa's Challenge.* Surprisingly little was known about cheetahs when Adamson began her studies. In 1976 Adamson began raising a leopard cub that she had named Penny. Although Penny was by nature solitary and secretive, she brought Adamson to see her cubs when they were only a few days old. The story of finding a habitat and reintroducing Penny into the wild is described in Adamson's book *Queen of Shaba.*

Adamson received numerous awards for her wildlife preservation work, and her paintings were exhibited throughout the world. On January 3, 1980, at age 70, Adamson was

Books by Joy Adamson

Born Free: A Lioness of Two Worlds **(1960)** The Adamsons raise Elsa, the orphaned lion cub.

Forever Free **(1962)** The story of Elsa's cubs after her death.

The Spotted Sphinx **(1969)** Adamson's story about raising her cheetah Pippa.

Queen of Shaba: The Story of an African Leopard **(1980)** Adamson raises Penny, a leopard, and then sets her free.

murdered by a domestic employee she had dismissed. Nine years later, at age 83, George Adamson was shot while driving to the rescue of a German woman being attacked by Somali thieves. Joy Adamson and her husband are remembered as prophets of the green (environmental) movement. They stimulated concern for animals and for the planet that humans and animals share.

Where to learn more

Adamson, Joy, *The Searching Spirit: An Autobiography,* Harcourt Brace, 1979.

Cass, Carolyn, *Joy Adamson: Behind the Mask,* Weidenfeld and Nicholson, 1992.

House, Adrian, *The Great Safari: The Lives of George and Joy Adamson,* William Morrow, 1993.

Jane Addams

Born September 6, 1860
Cedarville, Illinois
Died May 21, 1935
Chicago, Illinois
American social worker
Founded Hull House

"In time we came to define a settlement as an institution attempting to learn from life itself."

I n 1931 Jane Addams won the Nobel Peace Prize with educator and fellow activist Nicolas Murray Butler. A social reformer, Addams founded Hull House in Chicago, a settlement house (community center) where the desperately poor people of the neighborhood could get medical and social assistance. Seeking social justice, Addams worked with other activists in getting pioneer welfare laws passed, including the first juvenile court law and an eight-hour workday for women. She was also a well-known pacifist (peace worker) and became a dedicated international leader in the peace movement.

Inspired by her father

Addams was born in Cedarville, Illinois, only seven months before the Civil War started in 1860. Her mother died when she was two years old, and Addams was raised by her father, John Addams. He was a successful businessman and politician who helped build Cedarville into a thriving community. A Quaker, he believed in the ideals of hard work, achievement, democracy, and equality, and he lived a life of moral responsibility and purpose.

Addams was torn because of these teachings. She too believed it essential to do something important with her life, yet she grew up in a society that gave women the single role of homemaker. Even though her father encouraged her education, he believed its purpose was to make her a better wife and mother. Addams, however, desired more and enrolled in nearby Rockford College in 1877. Upon her graduation in 1881, she planned to attend Women's Medical College in Philadelphia, Pennsylvania, and later work as a doctor among the poor.

Finds direction unexpectedly

These plans changed when a mysterious illness struck Addams. An unknown back ailment forced her to drop out of college at the end of her first year. She underwent an operation and was confined to bed for six months. After recovering her health, she went to Europe to decide what to do with her life. Troubled by the dismal conditions of the poor in many European cities, Addams found a ray of hope at Toynbee Hall in England, where she discovered what could be done to help the poor. Founded by English clergyman Samuel Barnett in 1884, Toynbee Hall, the forerunner of the community center, was the very first settlement house. There Addams witnessed many people receiving the bare necessities of life–food, shelter, and clothing–which would otherwise be unattainable. She watched spirits soar and a sense of camaraderie grow as people worked together.

The Industrial Revolution and the poor

The Industrial Revolution took place in America in the years immediately following the Civil War. The boom of machines and manufacturing depended on cheap, plentiful workers, and millions of European immigrants swarmed into American cities to get the work. By the mid-1800s Western Europe and the Northeast United States were industrialized. By 1890, 80 percent of the people living in Chicago were immigrants or children of immigrants. Most cities, however, had neither the resources nor the will to handle the rapid population growth. Housing for many newcomers meant slums, places where poverty and hopelessness were concentrated. Tensions increased as people of different ethnic groups found their customs, languages, and lifestyles in conflict.

Addams and children sitting on the steps at Hull House.

Addams returned to America determined to achieve similar improvements. On September 8, 1889, she and Ellen Gates Starr opened Hull House on Halsted Street in the middle of Chicago's worst immigrant slum. By living at the center, Addams and her fellow reformers believed they could better understand the problems of the poor. Hull House offered the people of the surrounding neighborhood hot lunches, child care services, English-language classes, and parties. Addams tried to develop the idea of a neighborhood spirit by encouraging the immigrants to work together to do what they could to improve the conditions of their neighborhood. She also petitioned the city government to pave streets and to build public baths, parks, and playgrounds.

Seeks national reform

Local activities to improve social conditions soon spread to state and national levels. Community centers sprang up across America. Hull House became a meeting place for intellectuals and reformers who investigated every social problem confronting the country. National campaigns were developed for issues such as women's suffrage (the right to vote) and labor rights of women and children. Addams gave lectures and wrote articles and books detailing the work performed at the center. Her book *Twenty Years at Hull-House,* published in 1910, did much to promote her work. In 1911 the National Federation of Settlements and Neighborhood Centers was established, and Addams served as its first president.

When World War I (1914-1918) began, Addams became an outspoken member of the pacifist (peace) movement. The following year she and other peace-minded women founded the Women's Peace Party, which sought a peaceful end to the war and worked to establish a permanent international peacekeeping organization. National pride was high during and after the war, and pacifists were criticized for their activities. Undeterred, Addams went on to organize the Women's International League for Peace and Freedom to study, publicize, and help abolish the political, social, economic, and psychological causes of war and to build peace and respect for freedom. She served as its president until her death.

Addams also led in the women's suffrage movement to gain for women the right to vote. For her work toward peace, Addams and fellow activist Nicholas Murray Butler received the Nobel Peace Prize in 1931. Four year later she died of cancer in Chicago.

Settlement house

A settlement house differed from a social welfare agency in that its purpose was to improve life in the surrounding neighborhood instead of simply providing services. Gradually local and state governments and other organizations took over the functions of the settlement house, such as running kindergartens and health care clinics and providing educational and recreational activities for neighborhood residents and workers.

Where to learn more

Gleiter, Jan, *Jane Addams,* Raintree, 1988.

Kent, Deborah, *Jane Addams and Hull House,* Childrens Press, 1992.

Kitredge, Mary, *Jane Addams,* Chelsea House, 1988.

James, Edward T., editor, *Notable American Women: A Biographical Dictionary,* volume I, Belknap Press, 1975.

McPherson, Stephanie, *Peace and Bread: The Story of Jane Addams,* Carolrhoda Books, 1993.

Joan Aiken

Born September 4, 1924
Rye, Sussex, England
British science fiction writer
Writes fictional history

British author Joan Aiken, who began publishing fiction for young readers in 1953, is known for her critically acclaimed horror and suspense stories for younger readers. She won the Edgar Allan Poe Award for best juvenile mystery for her novel *Night Fall.*

She also began publishing adult fiction in the mid-1960s. Her work for adults ranges from horror to historical fiction, including *Mansfield Revisited,* her sequel to *Mansfield Park,* a novel by early nineteenth-century British author Jane Austen.

Her best-known work is the series of novels–beginning with *The Wolves of Willoughby Chase*–set in the reigns of the fictional nineteenth-century English kings James III and Richard IV. Praised by critics for her lively imagination, complicated plots, and humorous characters, Aiken has often been compared to Charles Dickens, the nineteenth-century British writer who used the same techniques.

"I knew I was going to be a writer like Conrad, like Martin, whose books could be seen around the house."

Books by Joan Aiken

The Wolves of Willoughby Chase (**1962**) A young girl and her cousin are left with a cruel governess. After being sent to an orphanage, the two girls must escape and find their way home.

Black Hearts in Battersea (**1964**) Presents the adventures of orphan girl Dido Twite. The sequel to *The Wolves*.

Bridle the Wind (**1983**) Running from an evil abbot, Felix escapes with Juan, who turns out to be a girl.

The Last Slice of Rainbow (**1985**) A collection of nine tales, including one about a tree that sends love letters to a young woman.

Dido and Pa (**1986**) Kidnapped by her father, a girl is called into service by a group who hope to overthrow the king, placing an impostor in his place.

Begins writing at early age

Aiken's father–the American-born poet Conrad Aiken–and her Canadian mother moved to England, where Aiken was born in 1924, because they believed schooling there would be better for Aiken's older siblings. However, Aiken received her early education at home from her mother. By the time Aiken was four years old, her parents had divorced and her mother had married another writer, Martin Armstrong. Aiken knew from an early age that she, too, would be a writer. From the time she was five years old, she continuously kept notebooks filled with her poems and stories. An avid reader, she especially liked Rudyard Kipling's Jungle books, Walter de la Mare's *Peacock Pie*, E. Nesbit's stories, and Frances Hodgson Burnett's *A Little Princess*.

Goes to boarding school

When Aiken was 12, her parents sent her to boarding school at Wychwood near Oxford, England. Although the school's bleak environment at first came as a shock to young

Aiken, she later recalled liking the competitive spirit she found there: "In no time I was devoting all my energy to getting the highest marks in class, getting parts in school plays, getting poems into the school magazine, being elected form [class] representative, and so on." Before Aiken left Wychwood, the school merged with Oxford High School due to the hardships of World War II. Set adrift in the larger school population and ill with a swollen neck gland, Aiken began to have trouble with her schoolwork, then failed the entrance exams for Oxford University. She took a clerical job with the British Broadcasting Corporation (BBC), although she admitted in an interview: "What I really wanted was to marry a rich man who would support me in the country while I wrote books."

Writes to pay debts

Bored with working at the BBC, Aiken took a job at the United Nations Information Office in London. There she met Ronald Brown, and she married him in 1945. In the meantime she continued writing. She sold two children's stories to the BBC and some poems to the magazine *Abinger Chronicle*. Aiken also completed a children's novel and entered it in a contest, which she didn't win. While she raised her two children, John and Elizabeth, more of her short stories were accepted by magazines. In 1953 she published her first book of short stories for children, *All You've Ever Wanted, and Other Stories*. She followed that book two years later with *More Than You Bargained For, and Other Stories,* another children's book.

Then Aiken's husband died of cancer, and she had several debts to pay and two children to support. She took a job as a story editor with *Argosy* magazine and supplemented her income by selling short stories. She got a literary agent, but then fired her because she thought that Aiken would succeed only by writing short fiction. Instead Aiken revised the novel she had entered in the contest, and the book was published in 1960 as *The Kingdom and the Cave.* Then in 1962 she wrote *The Wolves of Willoughby Chase,* which earned critical acclaim.

Creates fictional histories

The Wolves of Willoughby Chase is a story about a young girl and her cousin who are left with a cruel governess. After being sent to an orphanage, the two girls must escape and find their way home. A hit with readers, *The Wolves of Willoughby Chase* was also popular among reviewers, who praised the story's alternative history. In the second book of the series, *Black Hearts in Battersea,* Aiken introduces the dynamic orphan girl Dido Twite. This sequel was praised for its colorful language and its humorous tone.

For the next 20 years Aiken fabricated fictional history in books such as *Night Birds on Nantucket, The Cuckoo Tree,* and *The Stolen Lake.* In *Dido and Pa,* a 1986 addition to the series, the main character is kidnapped by her own father and taken to London. There she is called into service by the Hanoverians, a dynasty that once ruled Britain and hoped to rule again by overthrowing King Richard IV and putting an impostor on the throne. Several reviewers applauded Aiken's rich cast of characters and her thoughtful recreation of nineteenth-century London.

Felix and Juan and Other Stories

In the mid-1960s, Aiken realized her longtime ambition of publishing books for adults. Some of her adult novels, such as *The Smile of the Stranger, The Weeping Ash,* and *The Girl from Paris,* are set in historical times at her English home, the Hermitage in Petworth, West Sussex. Of her acclaimed *Mansfield Revisited,* Aiken explained in an interview: "It was different from writing any of the others. I did it very carefully with a copy of [lexicographer Samuel] Johnson's dictionary to make sure I wasn't using words that weren't in use during that time. I re-read Jane Austen at least once a year, so her style is very much in my ear. I read all the biographies of her that I could lay my hands on."

As a general rule, Aiken likes to alternate between writing for young readers and for adults. Among Aiken's other books for young readers, her stories about half-English, half-

Spanish Felix Brooke, set in early-nineteenth-century Europe, are among the author's favorites. In *Go Saddle the Sea,* the main character, Felix, who is mistreated by his Spanish grandfather, embarks on a series of adventures as he searches for his other distant relatives in England. When he encounters his English family, however, he discovers that they are just as disagreeable as those he left behind in Spain.

Bridle the Wind takes up with Felix when he decides to return to his Spanish grandfather. He gets shipwrecked on the coast of France, loses his memory, and finds himself working in a monastery ruled by a sinister abbot. Felix and Juan, who–he eventually discovers–is really a girl, escape from the community. Then he and Juan–renamed Juana–reunite several years later in *The Teeth of the Gale.* Juana, who is preparing to become a nun in a French convent, calls upon Felix to help rescue a group of children from an old castle atop a 200-foot crag.

Writes plays

Aiken has also written plays for young readers, including *Winterthing* and *The Mooncusser's Daughter,* poetry collections such as *The Skin Spinners,* and several short story anthologies. *The Last Slice of Rainbow,* published in 1985, contains nine tales, many of which Aiken spices with a bit of fantasy. Included in the collection are stories about a girl who can read other people's minds, a princess who is cursed with hair that continually scolds her, and a tree that sends love letters to a young woman.

Since marrying American painter and teacher Julius Goldstein in 1976, Aiken has divided her time between West Sussex and her husband's native New York City. She continues to write, and she and her older sister Jane, who is also a writer, review one another's work before they submit their manuscripts for publication.

Where to learn more

Aiken, Joan, "Writing Ghost Stories," *The Writer,* February 1994, p. 9.

Blishen, Edward, review of *Dido and Pa, Times Literary Supplement,* November 28, 1986, p. 1343.

Craig, Patricia, "The Elements of Adventure," *Times Literary Supplement,* May 6, 1988, p. 513.

Dooley, Susan, review of *Dido and Pa, Washington Post Book World,* November 9, 1986, p. 18.

Eliza's Daughter (review), *Publisher's Weekly,* May 16, 1994, p. 49.

Hirsch, Diana C., review of *The Haunting of Lamb House, School Library Journal,* May 1993.

Wawn, Andrew, review of *The Last Slice of Rainbow, Times Literary Supplement,* November 29, 1985, p. 1360.

Madeleine Albright

Born May 15, 1937
Prague, Czechoslovakia

Czechoslovakian-born
American public servant

U.S. ambassador to
the United Nations

I n 1992 President-elect Bill Clinton nominated Madeleine Albright to serve as the U.S. ambassador to the United Nations (U.N.), a post he intended to elevate to cabinet level. A specialist in Russian and East European affairs who had served as foreign affairs adviser to top Democratic officials, she became the first–and only–foreign-born member of President Clinton's cabinet. She also became the only woman in the U.N. Security Council and only the second woman to serve as a U.N. ambassador.

"It's a great thrill to represent the United States. And I'm sure that whether you're male or female, you have the same feeling when you are representing the most powerful country in the world."

Early life

Albright was born Maria Jana Korbel on May 15, 1937, in Prague, Czechoslovakia, one of three children of Josef and Ann Speeglova Korbel. After the family moved to the United States her mother re-christened her Madeleine. Albright once described herself in a *Los Angeles Times* interview as "the little blond girl in the newsreels who would be handing flowers to arriving diplomats." Her father, a pre-World War II Czechoslovakian diplomat, fled the Communist takeover of Czechoslovakia in 1948. After family members were granted U.S. political asylum, Korbel became a professor at the University of Denver in Denver, Colorado.

Changes career goals

Albright graduated with honors from Wellesley College in Wellesley, Massachusetts, in 1959. Three days later she married Joseph Albright, a member of the Alicia Patterson newspaper family, whom she had met while they were both students in New England. At first Albright thought she would become a journalist. In fact, she had started as a reporter with the *Rolla Daily News* in Missouri before moving to Chicago with her husband. While she was working at the newspaper, however, an editor for a competing paper called her "Honey" and advised her to find a career more suitable for a woman. Albright later told an interviewer, "I listened to him and gave up the idea–I would fight it, now, of course–but I think I'm better at what I do now than I would have been as a journalist."

Becomes political adviser

The Albrights had three children who were still young when the family moved to Washington, D.C., in the mid-1970s. While living in Washington, Albright completed a doctorate degree in 1976 by commuting to Columbia University in New York City, where she also had received a master's degree in 1968. Immediately after earning her doctorate she became a legislative assistant to Democratic Senator Edmund S. Muskie. Two years later she joined the national security staff of President Jimmy Carter, working as a legislative liaison with former Columbia University professor Zbigniew Brzezinski, who was Carter's national security adviser.

Expands to foreign policy

In 1982 Albright joined the faculty of Georgetown University in Washington, D.C. The following year she and her

Albright addressing an emergency session of the United Nations Security Council.

husband were divorced. During the 1984 election campaign she served as an adviser to Democratic presidential candidate Walter F. Mondale and his vice presidential running mate Geraldine A. Ferraro, who failed to win the general election. In 1988 Albright was a principal adviser to Democratic candidate Michael Dukakis. It was widely presumed that she would have been offered a high-ranking job if he had won. After Dukakis's defeat Albright became president of the Center for National Policy, a Democratic "think tank," or policy advisory organization. She continued running a foreign policy "salon"–an informal gathering of top foreign policy experts–at her Georgetown home.

Appointed U.N. ambassador

In 1992 President Clinton nominated Albright as the U.S. ambassador to the United Nations. The nomination was approved by Congress, and many people praised Clinton's choice. Albright's foreign affairs specialties are Eastern European and Russian, and she has consistently advocated a more active U.S. role in promoting democracy in those parts of the world. She has long been acquainted with many of the leaders of newly freed countries in Eastern Europe and the former Soviet Union. For instance, Albright became an adviser to Vaclav Havel when he was elected president of Czechoslovakia following the "Velvet Revolution," or the peaceful overthrow of the communist regime in that country, in 1989. In an interview with the *Los Angeles Times,* Albright said that being U.S. ambassador to the U.N. was "the luckiest and most fascinating thing that's ever happened to me, because it is a moment when the United States government believes that working within the United Nations is good and positive and useful."

Upon her appointment Albright was thrust immediately into the most pressing issues of the time. She discussed her feelings about being the only woman on the U.N. Security Council and the second American woman to be an ambassador to the U.N. "It's a great thrill to represent the United States," she said. "And I'm sure that whether you're male or female, you have the same feeling when you are representing the most powerful country in the world.... But there is an interesting sense about being the only woman. There's a sense doubly I think, a tremendous sense of exhilaration about being a woman. There's no question about that. Then the opposite sense which is wishing there were more women there [in the U.N.]."

Where to learn more

Christian Science Monitor, December 28, 1992.

Los Angeles Times, May 2, 1993; December 23, 1992.

New York Times, December 22, 1992; December 23, 1992

Time, October 31, 1994.

U.S. News & World Report, February 13, 1995.

Washington Post, December 23, 1993; December 29, 1992.

Alicia Alonso

Born December 21, 1917(?)
Havana, Cuba
Cuban ballerina
Established Ballet Nacional de Cuba
(National Ballet of Cuba)

Alicia Alonso has been fascinating audiences with her ballet performances for more than 50 years. The winner of numerous awards, Alonso is a world-class dance artist. She broke cold war barriers to dance *Giselle,* and she even went on to perform the same piece when she was blind. She brought ballet to Cuba when she established the Ballet Nacional de Cuba (National Ballet of Cuba) as well as a national ballet school.

Alonso was born Alicia Ernestina de la Caridad del Cobre Martinez on December 21 (the year of her birth has been variously listed as 1917, 1921, and 1922) in Havana, Cuba. Her father, Antonio Martinez, was a lieutenant in the Cuban army, and her mother, Ernestina Martinez, cared for their four children at home. Alonso took dancing lessons at the Sociedad Pro-Arte Musical (Society for Musical Art) and debuted at age 10 in *Sleeping Beauty,* the ballet by nineteenth-century Russian composer Piotr Ilyich Tchaikovsky.

"I live when I dance. I live not just for myself. When I'm on stage with my dancers, I live with them. It is life."

Moves to the United States

At the Sociedad she met Fernando Alonso, who was also a dancer, and they were married on February 19, 1937. The couple moved to New York City, and Alicia trained at the School of American Ballet. Although she worked with some of the best private teachers of classical ballet, she did not yet begin her ballet career. Her first stage performances were as a tap dancer in musical comedies in the late 1930s. She joined the American Ballet Caravan as a soloist by 1939, then signed with the American Ballet Theatre, where she was given solo parts.

Vision problems hinder career

Alonso was well on her way to a successful career when she began having severe problems with her vision. When her retinas (the inner lining of the eyes) became detached, she was temporarily blinded. Three operations restored her vision, but she was confined to bed for one year. She was forbidden to turn her head, laugh, or even cry. Yet Alonso never lost her passion for the ballet. She began to envision herself dancing, and by this technique she learned the movements of the lead role in *Giselle,* a ballet by nineteenth-century French composer Adolphe Adam. When the heavy bandages were removed, Alonso found she could see, but she also found that she had to learn how to walk again. It was not long before Alonso was dancing the very role she had rehearsed over and over again in her mind as she lay blind in bed. At the Metropolitan Opera House in 1943, she danced *Giselle* in place of a dancer who was ill. Her performance was praised by critics, and Alonso eventually became famous for her unique interpretation of *Giselle.* Three years later she was made principal dancer.

Forms ballet company in Cuba

In 1948 Alonso returned to Cuba to found her own ballet company, the Ballet Alicia Alonso, which provided American Ballet Theatre dancers with work while inspiring potential dancers and ballet enthusiasts alike throughout South America. Alonso became concerned, however, that too many of her dancers were non-Cubans. So in 1950, with government and private support, she opened the Alicia Alonso Academy of Ballet in Havana, which soon became a showcase for Cuban talent. By 1956, however, Alonso had to disband the company. Under the government of President Fulgencio Batista, the company suffered from declining annual subsidies, so Alonso left Cuba to dance elsewhere.

Embarks on tour behind iron curtain

For the next three years Alonso worked as a guest artist in Monte Carlo, Monaco, with the Ballet Russe de Monte Carlo, and during that time she was invited to dance in the Soviet Union. This highly unusual invitation demonstrated the respect Alonso had earned throughout the world. No Western dancer had ever been asked to perform behind the Communist "iron curtain" during the cold war (when the Soviet Union and the countries of the West maintained a hostile peace in the aftermath of World War II). Then Alonso returned to the United States. Following the Cuban revolution in 1959, Batista was overthrown and Fidel Castro assumed power, and Alonso decided to return to Cuba. Because so many Cubans were fleeing their own country to live in America, many people believed Alonso was making a mistake. Nevertheless Alonso was determined to become part of the revolution and make important contributions to her people now that Batista's regime was out of power.

Founds Ballet Nacional de Cuba

Castro gave Alonso $200,000 to reopen her school and start the Ballet Nacional de Cuba, which was given official status and guaranteed backing by the federal government. Within a short time the company had over 100 dancers and dance schools throughout the country. Every child was promised a free education in Cuba, and any serious and talented student could receive ballet instruction. Choreographers created original works for the company, and the ballet per-

Alonso, at age 72, performing Swan Lake during the American Ballet Theater's Fiftieth Anniversary Gala at the Metropolitan Opera House in New York City.

formed for all kinds of audiences, poor and rich alike, in parks, schools, and even factories.

Overcomes political and personal obstacles

For several years the Ballet Nacional de Cuba was prohibited from touring in the United States because its govern-

Alicia Alonso   28

ment was a Communist regime. Instead Alonso took the Ballet Nacional de Cuba to other Communist countries, including the People's Republic of China, Mongolia, North Vietnam, and countries in Central and South America. It was not until 1971 that the Ballet Nacional de Cuba could make a North American tour. Audiences were in awe of Alonso's performance in *Giselle,* especially considering that the dancer was by now almost completely blind. She was led to her position on the stage, and the bright spotlights helped her keep in position. Afterwards she followed a voice off the stage. Her vision was restored by surgeons in Barcelona, Spain, in 1972, and she was well enough to perform again by 1975.

Role extends beyond dance

Since 1958 Alonso has been involved in many other activities. She is a member of the World Council for Peace and has served as vice president of the National Union of Cuban Writers and Artists. She also shares the work of all Cubans–she fulfills her agricultural duties in the coffee fields, as do the other members of the company. After her divorce from Fernando Alonso in 1977, she married writer and lawyer Pedro Simon. During the 1990s, again nearly blind and past the age of 70, Alonso appeared in special performances in the United States and Chile.

Where to learn more

Arnold, Sandra Martín, *Alicia Alonso: First Lady of the Ballet,* Walker and Co., 1993.

Dance, August 1990; November 1991.

New Leader, March 5, 1990.

Marian Anderson

Born February 17, 1902
Philadelphia, Pennsylvania
Died April 1993
Portland, Oregon
African American opera singer
First black American to perform at the White House and the Metropolitan Opera

"I hadn't set out to change the world in any way. Whatever I am, it is a culmination of the goodwill of people who, regardless of anything else, saw me as I am, and not as somebody else."

Marian Anderson, whose voice had a range of three octaves, is remembered as one of the greatest American contraltos (a singer with a voice range between tenor and mezzo-soprano). She had a series of "firsts" to her credit, among them being the first black American to sing at the White House and to perform with the Metropolitan Opera Company of New York.

Early life and training

Anderson was born February 17, 1902, in Philadelphia, Pennsylvania. Her father sold coal and ice, and her mother, who had been a schoolteacher before marrying, took in laundry and did housekeeping to make ends meet. Anderson's earliest vocal training came at Philadelphia's Union Baptist Church, where she began singing spirituals and hymns in the junior choir at age six. She debuted when she was eight, performing "The Lord Is My Shepherd," for which she received

50 cents. Later Anderson earned money from doing chores and, with the help of her father, bought a piano from a pawn shop. Her father died when she was twelve, and five years later, her mother contracted a serious case of the flu, leaving young Marian to take over support of the family.

Anderson came up against blatant racial prejudice when she was 15 and she applied for admission to a music school. Told "We don't take colored," Anderson was shaken, because in her integrated neighborhood the term "colored" was never used. Instead she took voice lessons with local teachers. When she was 18, however, she had outgrown her teachers but could not afford the more expensive training she needed. Members of Union Baptist Church came to her rescue and started a "Marian Anderson Fund" to hire Giuseppe Boghetti, a famous voice teacher.

Contest winner

Encouraged by Anderson's appearance at Town Hall in New York City in 1925, Boghetti entered her into a contest. Competing against 300 other singers, Anderson took first prize and won the opportunity to sing at Lewisohn Stadium with the New York Philharmonic Orchestra. In spite of her triumph, Anderson's career did not advance as expected because her concerts stayed mainly in the African American community. However, in summer 1929 she sailed to England to study with other vocal teachers.

Triumph in Europe

When she came back to the States, Anderson gave a series of successful concerts. After a 1931 concert in Chicago, she was approached by a representative from the Julius Rosenwald Fund, a foundation funding higher education opportunities for black Americans. She was given a Rosenwald scholarship, which allowed her to travel to Germany to study with vocal coach Michael Raucheisen. Anderson enjoyed success in Europe: in 1933 she toured for a year and sang 108

concerts in Europe and Russia. By the time Anderson returned to the United States, she had become an acclaimed sensation in European capitals.

In December 1935 Anderson gave another recital at Town Hall. She had fractured a bone in her left foot on the ocean liner before she landed, so during the concert she hid the cast beneath her gown. The performance was a great success, and critics proclaimed her the "new high priestess of song." In 1936 she sang for President Franklin D. Roosevelt at the White House, where she suffered her only attack of stage fright. Anderson was later invited back to the White House to perform for King George and Queen Elizabeth of England. She made several cross-country tours and was soon booking engagements two years in advance. Every appearance was immediately sold out; one year she covered 26,000 miles–the longest tour in concert history–giving 70 concerts in five months.

Victory over racial discrimination

In 1939 the Daughters of the American Revolution (DAR) unintentionally made Anderson known to millions of Americans. The DAR, a nonprofit organization of women that conducts historical, educational, and patriotic activities, refused to let Anderson sing an April 9 concert in Constitution Hall in Washington, D.C. A huge outcry ensued, and first lady **Eleanor Roosevelt** (see entry) resigned her DAR membership in protest. The federal government then gave Anderson permission to give a free outdoor concert on Easter Sunday at the Lincoln Memorial. A crowd of 75,000 attended, and the radio audience numbered into the millions. Anderson opened with her rendition of "My Country 'tis of Thee."

Later that year Mrs. Roosevelt presented to Anderson the Spingarn Medal, the prestigious award given annually by the National Association for the Advancement of Colored People (NAACP) to an outstanding black American. In 1941 Anderson received the Bok Award, with a prize of $10,000, from Philadelphia, her hometown. She started the Marian Anderson awards–cash scholarships given each year to 10 aspiring young singers regardless of race or creed. In 1942 the DAR again refused to let Anderson sing in Constitution Hall. She had demanded that the audience for the concert, a war benefit, not be segregated. In 1943 she finally sang at Constitution Hall for a China Relief Fund benefit. That same year Anderson married Orpheus Fisher, an architectural engineer, whom she had known for more than 20 years. In 1948 she underwent a dangerous operation for removal of a cyst from her esophagus. After a successful recovery, Anderson toured Europe.

Opera debut and later career

Anderson had once expressed a desire to sing in an opera, but she did not realize her dream until January 7, 1955, at the age of 52. Her operatic debut took place at the Metropolitan Opera House in New York, where she sang the role of Ulrica in the Verdi opera *Un ballo in maschera* (*The Masquerade Ball*). She was the first black American ever to sing at the Metropolitan Opera Company, then 72 years old.

Anderson paved the way at the Metropolitan Opera for other well-known black singers such as Robert McFerrin, Gloria Davy, Grace Bumbry, **Leontyne Price** *(see entry), Jessye Norman, and* **Kathleen Battle** *(see entry).*

Over the years Anderson added to her accomplishments. She sang at presidential inaugurations for Dwight D. Eisenhower and John F. Kennedy. She also served as a U.S. delegate to the United Nations and made a 40,000-mile tour of the Far East. That tour was filmed by CBS-TV and sponsored by the U.S. State Department. On Easter Sunday 1965 Anderson gave her farewell concert with a program of classical music and spirituals at Carnegie Hall in New York. Her husband of 40 years, Orpheus Fisher, died in 1983. Anderson died in April 1993 in Portland, Oregon.

Where to learn more

Anderson, Marian, *My Lord, What a Morning,* Viking, 1956.

McKissack, Pat, *Marian Anderson: A Great Singer,* Enslow, 1991.

Tedards, Anne, *Marian Anderson,* Chelsea House, 1988.

Maya Angelou

Born April 4, 1928
St. Louis, Missouri

African American writer

Chronicled her life story in a series of
best-selling autobiographies

The first poet since Robert Frost in 1964 to read a poem at the inauguration of a president of the United States, Maya Angelou has produced work that has been nominated for numerous awards. A woman of many talents, she has published autobiographies, poems, plays, and films, and is one of America's literary treasures. Nevertheless, as she wrote in her first autobiography, *I Know Why the Caged Bird Sings,* "The fact that the adult American Negro female emerges as a formidable character is often met with amazement, distaste and even belligerence."

"Courage is the most important virtue, because without courage you can't have the other virtues."

Suffered traumatic childhood experience

Angelou was born Marguerite Johnson on April 4, 1928, in St. Louis, Missouri. After Angelou's parents were divorced when she was three years old, she and her older brother, Bailey, went to live with their maternal grandmother. A country grocer in Stamps, Arkansas, Angelou's grandmother taught the

Autobiographical Works

I Know Why the Caged Bird Sings **(1970)** Angelou's childhood memories of growing up in the rural South.

Gather Together in My Name **(1974)** Angelou continues her life story by describing what happened when she left her mother's house in her late teens and ventured out on her own with her baby son.

Singin' and Swingin' and Gettin' Merry Like Christmas **(1976)** In her third autobiographical book Angleou gives an account of her passage into adulthood during the 1950s. After a brief marriage she began performing as an actress, singer, and dancer.

The Heart of a Woman **(1981)** Angelou tells more about her life (from 1957 to 1962), which includes living on a Sausalito houseboat, her common-law marriage, and her son entering college.

All God's Children Need Traveling Shoes **(1986)** Angelou concentrates on the four years she spent in Ghana, Africa, looking for her roots and discovering the differences between Africans and herself as an African American.

children the importance of religion, work, and courage in the face of bigotry. Angelou's growing confidence was destroyed, however, when, at age eight, she visited her mother in St. Louis, where she was raped by her mother's boyfriend. The resulting trial was traumatic, and then the man was murdered (she suspected that her uncles killed him). Afterward Angelou refused to talk for five years.

Performing artist first

By the time Angelou was in her early twenties, she had been a Creole cook, the first black woman to be a streetcar conductor in San Francisco, a dancer, a madam, and a single parent. When she was in her late twenties and early thirties, she emerged as a successful singer and actress, performing in

Movie Adaptations

Georgia, Georgia, **(1972)** A black female entertainer on tour in Sweden falls in love with a white photographer. Conflict arises when her traveling companion tries to break up the couple.

I Know Why the Caged Bird Sings **(1979)** A black writer's memories of growing up in the rural South during the 1930s.

Poetic Justice **(1993)** Features Angelou's verse and stars singer Janet Jackson as Justice, a woman who gives up college plans to follow a career in cosmetology after her boyfriend's brutal murder.

the 1954 production of *Porgy and Bess,* which toured Canada, Europe, and Israel. Angelou next appeared in off-Broadway productions such as *Calypso Heatwave, The Blacks,* and *Cabaret for Freedom.*

Civil rights activist

In the early 1960s Angelou joined the civil rights movement and worked for Dr. Martin Luther King, Jr. Then she moved to Africa and worked as a journalist in Cairo, Egypt, at the English-language weekly *Arab Observer* and in Accra, Ghana, at the *African Review.* Angelou also taught dance and music at the University of Ghana. Upon her return to the United States in 1966, she resumed work in theater, writing 10 programs about African influences on American life for National Educational Television.

Writes autobiography

Angelou began writing her autobiography after some friends, including the author James Baldwin, heard her telling stories about her childhood in Arkansas, Missouri, and California. The story of her life up to age 16 and ending with the

birth of her son, Guy, was published in 1970 with the title *I Know Why the Caged Bird Sings.* The book was a great critical and commercial success. Along with the traumas of her early years, it recounts humorous events as well as the young Angelou's coming to self-awareness. She followed this book with four other autobiographical volumes.

College professor

Since the 1970s Angelou has had faculty appointments at a number of universities across the United States, including the University of California at Los Angeles, California State University at Sacramento, Kansas State University at Manhattan, and Wichita State University at Wichita. In 1981 Angelou moved back to the South, accepting a lifetime appointment as a professor of American studies at Wake Forest University in Wake Forest, North Carolina. Her books have earned her nominations for prestigious awards such as the Pulitzer Prize, the Tony Awards, and the National Book Award.

Continuing contributions

At the inauguration of President Bill Clinton in 1993, Angelou read a poem, becoming the first poet to appear at this event since Robert Frost recited his poetry at the inauguration of President John F. Kennedy. For the occasion Angelou composed "On the Pulse of Morning," and it appeared in newspapers throughout the world the following day. Dedicated to a nation of immigrants, the poem captures the multicultural spirit of the United States and was later published in book form.

Recent poetry and inspirational writing

"I Shall Not Be Moved" (1990)

"Lessons in Living" (1993)

"On the Pulse of Morning" (1993)

Where to learn more

Angelou, Maya, *I Know Why the Caged Bird Sings,* Bantam, 1988, pp. 35-36.

King, Sarah E., *Maya Angelou: Greeting the Morning,* Millbrook Press, 1994.

Essence, December 1992; August 1993.

New York Times, January 20, 1993; January 21, 1993; January 30, 1993; April 2, 1993; July 23, 1993.

People, January 18, 1993.

Virginia Apgar

Born June 7, 1909
Westfield, New Jersey

Died August 7, 1974
New York, New York

American physician
Developed the Apgar score

"Nobody,
but nobody,
is going to
stop breathing
on me."

In 1952 Virginia Apgar developed a test–known as the Apgar score–that revolutionized the diagnosis of birth defects. A method of determining a newborn baby's condition and chance for survival, the test is given within the first 60 seconds after birth. An anesthesiologist who had attended the births of more than 17,000 babies, Apgar devised the test to focus delivery room attention on babies who had previously been neglected, often with detrimental results.

Pursues active college life

Apgar was born on June 7, 1909, in Westfield, New Jersey, the daughter of Charles Apgar, a businessman and teacher of salesmanship, and Helen Clarke Apgar. After graduating from high school, she attended Mount Holyoke College in South Hadley, Massachusetts. There she demonstrated the remarkable energy that characterized her entire life. Besides being active in numerous intramural and varsity sports, she served on academic teams and reported for the school newspaper. She appeared in several college dramas and played violin in the orchestra—all the while putting herself through school by working at various jobs, such as opening the library every morning, taking care of a science lab, waiting tables, selling linens, and, as one observer noted, "catching stray cats for comparative anatomy classes."

Chooses a career field

She graduated from Mount Holyoke with a bachelor of science degree in 1929, then was admitted to Columbia University in New York City, where she earned a medical degree four years later. Planning to be a surgeon, Apgar served an internship in surgery at Presbyterian Hospital in New York City for two years. In 1936 she returned to Columbia as an instructor at the College of Physicians and Surgeons. Although she had initially trained for surgery, Apgar decided that the specialty of anesthesiology held more career opportunities for a female physician. So while teaching at Columbia, she served a residency in anesthesiology at Belleview Hospital in New York City. By 1949 Apgar had worked her way up through the academic ranks to become the first female physician ever made full professor at Columbia College of Physicians and Surgeons. Over the years she also advised students, helping them with personal and academic problems.

Gains international reputation

During Apgar's tenure as clinical director of anesthesiology at Columbia-Presbyterian Medical Center, she built an anesthesiology department that was reportedly one of the best in the world. Applying her usual energy and devotion, she maintained her teaching duties while conducting extensive research on prenatal care and teratology, the study of birth defects. Apgar published more than 50 articles on these subjects in medical journals. In 1952 she developed the test that came to be called the Apgar score, and her test revolutionized the diagnosis of birth defects. In 1959 Apgar was appointed

The Apgar score

The Apgar Score is a series of five tests given to all newborn infants three times within 10 minutes of birth. Using the letters of her last name, Virginia Apgar designed the test to evaluate the following vital signs of new life.

Appearance (color of the infant's skin). The skin should not show evidence of jaundice, or a blue or yellow tinge to the skin; there is also a problem if the infant is unusually pale.

Pulse (rate of heartbeat). The infant should have a quick heart beat.

Grimace (reflex or irritability). The doctor pricks the bottom of the infant's foot; if the infant grimaces (makes a face or cries), the reflexes are normal.

Activity (muscle tone). The doctor pushes back one of the infant's legs; if the infant shows resistance, muscle tone is normal.

Respiration (breathing rate). If the infant's breathing is regular, respiration is normal.

The baby is scored on the basis of these categories, each of which can receive zero to two points. A perfect score of 10 indicates an excellent chance for survival and a normal life. The average score is eight to 10 points. A score below three gives the infant a poor chance for survival or the possibility of grave abnormalities if the baby does survive the first critical weeks.

head of the division of congenital malformations (birth defects) at the National Foundation-March of Dimes in New York, then became director of basic research in 1967. Five years later she published a guide for pregnant women about prenatal care and the avoidance of abnormalities, entitled *Is My Baby All Right?*

Honored for achievements

In her later years Apgar was a lecturer at Cornell University in Ithaca, New York, and Johns Hopkins University in Baltimore, Maryland. She was also a consultant to the National Research Council and to various hospitals. For her work in diagnosing and preventing birth defects, she received a distinguished service award from the American Society of Anesthesiology in 1961 as well as numerous honorary degrees. In 1973 she was named senior vice president for medical affairs at the March of Dimes. Apgar died on August 7, 1974, in New York City.

Where to learn more

Apgar, Virginia, *Is My Baby All Right? A Guide to Birth Defects,* Trident Press, 1972.

Sicherman, Barbara, editor, *Notable American Women: The Modern Period,* Belknap Press, 1980.

Corazon Aquino

Born January 25, 1933
Tarlac, Philippines
Filipina political leader
Former president of the Philippines

"It was never my intention to seek the presidency of the Philippines. But sometimes life does not proceed as you expected it to. You must deal with the circumstances you're in."

Corazon Aquino, who became the first female president of the Phillipines, rode the tide of popular sentiment against President Ferdinand Marcos and won that country's 1986 presidential elections. Though she had not originally sought political office, Aquino was swept into it by her upbringing, the violent death of her husband, and the demands of her people.

On August 21, 1993, Aquino's husband, Filipino politician Benigno Aquino, was gunned down at the Manila airport in the Philippines. He was returning from exile in the United States, and his murder incited mass demonstrations against President Marcos. The funeral attracted over 1 million mourners in a 10-hour procession, and Aquino found herself the symbolic head of the growing anti-Marcos movement.

When President Marcos called for elections in November 1985, Aquino, previously a traditional wife and mother, was pressured to run for president. Though at first given little chance of winning, she received the support of the anti-Marcos forces and won the February 1986 election. Marcos then tried to deny the victory, but military insurrection and mass public demonstrations finally forced him to flee the country. Aquino's "people power" revolution, which had toppled the entrenched dictatorship, would turn out to be the easy part of her administration. Solving her country's very real political and economic problems would prove to be extremely difficult for the new president.

Born to a wealthy, political family

Aquino was born Maria Corazon (nicknamed Cory) Cojuangco on January 25, 1933, in Tarlac Province, north of Manila, in the Philippines. She was the sixth of eight children. Of Chinese, Malay, and Spanish ancestry, her family became the wealthiest in the province with sugar and banking holdings. Aquino's grandfather, father, and brother served in national office, giving the family national political power. Aquino attended an elite school in Manila before her parents sent her to the United States when she was 13. She attended Catholic schools in Philadelphia and New York City, graduating from Mount St. Vincent College in New York City in 1953 with a major in French.

During a summer vacation Corazon Aquino met her future husband, journalist Benigno Aquino. Like her, he came from a wealthy family in Tarlac Province. The young Filipina was a law student and was not interested in the young man at first, but dropped out of school to marry him in 1954. Benigno's political career skyrocketed when he became the youngest mayor, governor, and then senator in Philippine history. Corazon served as hostess at parties and gave birth to five children.

Benigno Aquino jailed

In a move to keep his political power in 1972, President Ferdinand Marcos declared martial law, placing the military in charge of the country. Then he extended his rule beyond the constitutional limit of two terms. The first person he jailed was the politician considered most likely be the next president–Benigno Aquino–on fake charges of murder, subversion, and firearms possession. Benigno spent the next seven and one-half years in prison. Corazon Aquino became her husband's link to the outside world, memorizing his messages and speeches and delivering them to the press. Fearful for her husband's life, she herself was subjected to frequent strip searches and other indignities. In 1980 U.S. president Jimmy Carter pressured President Marcos to release Benigno Aquino for heart surgery, and the Aquinos then moved to Boston, Massachusetts. After the surgery, Benigno worked on research projects at Harvard University. Corazon Aquino describes those years as the happiest of her life.

Husband's assassination drives Aquino into politics

In 1983, as opposition to President Marcos was mounting, the 50-year-old Benigno Aquino's supporters encouraged him to come home and lead the opposition. At the Manila airport on August 21, 1983, moments after arriving from the United States, Benigno was assassinated. The president formally blamed communists and appointed a commission to investigate, but Corazon Aquino called Marcos "the No. 1 suspect."

Vowing to continue her late husband's work, Aquino led the opposition to one-third of the parliamentary seats in 1984. To show he still had popular support, Marcos called for elections in February 1986. Aquino was pressured to run, even though she objected, "What do I know about being President?" When the Philippine courts overturned the convictions of her husband's murderers, she changed her mind. Her lack of campaign experience was readily apparent, but then Aquino abandoned her written speeches and began speaking from her heart. She presented herself as a moral alternative to Marcos's corruption.

Aquino's election called a democratic triumph

The election was held on February 7, 1986. Despite claims of Marcos officials stealing ballot boxes and intimidat-

Election significance

The significance of Corazon Aquino's victory over Ferdinand Marcos was that it showed an electoral democracy can work. President Marcos was a dictator who permitted the election to take place, because he assumed he could cheat to win. Through violence, fraud, vote buying, and ballot theft, Marcos had hoped to rig his re-election. Aquino had no way to stop Marcos's voter manipulation, yet independent polls and impartial ballot watchers showed Aquino easily winning in spite of his underhanded tactics. The day after the polls closed, Marcos declared himself a winner by a 54-46 percent margin. Aquino also declared victory and was sworn into office in a secret ceremony. The Filipino people never recognized Marcos's claim to victory. For several weeks there were riots in the streets and protests outside the lavish presidential mansion. Marcos's downfall came when he lost the support of military leaders. His departure put to an end a brutal dictatorship that had drained off the wealth of the country. Very little of the billions of dollars stolen by the Marcoses and other government officials was ever found.

ing voters, Aquino was winning. When Marcos sought to take the election and proclaim himself victor, his defense minister, Juan Ponce Enrile, and his deputy chief of staff, Fidel Ramos, defected to Aquino's side and barricaded themselves in the defense ministry building. Marcos sent in troops, but the soldiers were surrounded by Aquino's supporters. They retreated, and a few days later the defeated President Marcos and his wife, Imelda, fled in an American helicopter to Hawaii. Within an hour the United States recognized the Aquino government, and President Ronald Reagan proclaimed the Aquino election as "a triumph of democracy."

Survives repeated attempts on her life

Once the inauguration was a reality, Aquino experienced the difficulty of solving her country's overwhelming problems. As an offer of reconciliation, she released over 500 political prisoners and then freed 4 communist leaders. She spurned the opulent Malacanang Palace as a residence and

Aquino (left) being sworn in
as Filipino president. Doña
Aurora Aquino (center),
Benigno's mother, stands
by her side.

lived instead in a guest house. Aquino promised free enterprise, social justice, land reform, and an end to cronyism in the government (the practice of officials giving jobs to unqualified friends and associates). She endured a July 1986 coup attempt against her government. She came home from a September 1986 visit to the United States with $200 million in aid from the U.S. Congress.

Yet President Aquino found it difficult to change Filipino society for the better. Poverty and violence remained at high levels. Attempts to assassinate her continued with regularity, and one in August 1987 was nearly successful. Rebel troops mutinied, leaving 52 dead and 300 wounded after a battle in the streets of Manila. Aquino took a hard line against the rebels and managed to maintain order. But overpopulation, crime, inflation, and poverty continued to increase. When elections were held in 1992, the Filipino people were disillusioned with Aquino. There were several presidential candidates, including Imelda Marcos, the wife of the former dictator, but Aquino was not among them. She threw her support to Fidel Ramos, who won the election.

Where to learn more

Chua-Eoan, Howard, *Corazon Aquino,* Chelsea House, 1988.

Komisar, Lucy, *Corazon Aquino: The Story of a Revolution,* Braziller, 1987.

Lepthien, Emilie, *Corazon Aquino: President of the Philippines,* Childrens Press, 1987.

Nadel, Laurie, *Corazon Aquino: Journey to Power,* Julian Messner, 1987.

Elizabeth Arden

Born December 31, 1878?
Woodbridge, Ontario, Canada

Died October 18, 1966
New York, New York

Canadian-born American
businesswoman

Founder of a cosmetics company
and one of the most successful
entrepreneurs in the United States

"Nothing that costs only a dollar is worth having."

During the first half of the twentieth century great changes in feminine grooming were brought about by the popularity of motion pictures and the growth of the toiletries industry. At the forefront in creating change was Elizabeth Arden, an entrepreneur who developed less greasy makeups and creams. As women began to accept cosmetics, she introduced innovations such as lipsticks that matched skin coloring and clothing. By being on the ground floor of a new industry, Arden was able to build a financial empire, but it was her hard work and ability to turn ideas into products that made her a success.

Early life in poverty

Arden was born Florence Nightingale Graham in Woodbridge, Ontario, Canada, a village near Toronto. Her father was William Graham, a Scotsman, and her mother, Susan Tadd, was an Englishwoman from Cornwall. The Grahams had emigrated to Canada, worked as tenant farmers, and had five children, four girls and a boy (Arden was the third of four daughters). Susan Graham died when the children were still small and the family was poverty stricken. Arden had a number of low-paying jobs and few prospects for the future when she decided at the age of 30 to follow her brother to New York City.

Changes name to Arden

Arden's first job was as a clerical assistant with Eleanor Adair, who operated a beauty salon that gave facials. Arden, who had smooth facial skin that made her look ten years younger than she actually was, pressured Adair to teach her this new technique. She soon became expert at administering facials and was nicknamed "healing hands." Realizing she would never make money working for another person–one of the first signs of a true entrepreneur–Arden went into a partnership with a friend named Elizabeth Hubbard. The two women opened a salon at 509 Fifth Avenue, but soon fell to arguing and Hubbard left.

Now Arden had an opportunity to start a business of her own. With a small loan from her brother she refurbished the shop in an opulent style and had the front door painted red–the red door with a brass nameplate would later become the trademark of Elizabeth Arden cosmetics. Needing a name for her business, she took Arden from the poem "Enoch Arden" by nineteenth-century British poet Alfred Lord Tennyson. Since Elizabeth Hubbard's name was still on the front window in gold leaf, Arden decided she could save money by keeping Elizabeth and substituting Arden for Hubbard. Thus Florence Graham became Elizabeth Arden, although she never legally changed her name.

Travels to Paris

Despite the outbreak of World War I (1914-1918), Arden traveled to Paris in 1914 where she sampled facials in a number of salons, except that of Helena Rubenstein, who was

A passion for horse racing

Arden matched her success in business with a success in horse raising. As owner of Maine Chance Stables in Lexington, Kentucky, her horses won the top purses in the major races in 1945 with a total of $589,000. The next year the success of her horses resulted in a cover story in *Time,* and in 1947 her horse Jet Pilot won the 1947 Kentucky Derby. Arden even had trainers treat the thoroughbreds' sores with Arden's Eight Hour Cream. About racehorses and women Arden once said: "They must be petted and cared for the same way."

becoming her rival in the cosmetics industry and whom Arden referred to as "that woman." Arden had already started to use face makeup as part of her facials, and now she observed the effects produced with mascara and eye shadow. On her return to the United States she opened a shop in Washington, D.C., selling creams and cosmetics, and creating makeups for her costumers. It was here that she introduced Amoretta, a best-selling facial cream. As cosmetics gained in popularity Arden offered an array of services for personal grooming, such as hairdressing, diet, exercise, and clothing.

Business profitable

On November 29, 1915, Arden married Thomas Jenkins Lewis, a banker she had met a year earlier while applying for a loan. Lewis ran Arden's cosmetics business for 20 years (the cosmetics sales helped fund the operation of the less successful salons). The marriage worked well as a business arrangement, but in 1934 Arden divorced Lewis. In 1942 she married Prince Michael Evlanoff, a Russian, but this union lasted just two years. Catering to a rich clientele, she expanded her business interests by opening a health resort at Maine Chance Farm in Mount Vernon, Maine, followed by a second in Phoenix, Arizona, in 1947. Although Arden was a frequent traveler and used her name to sponsor charity balls, her business was the center of her life.

Worked all her life

Arden's career provided a model for all aspiring entrepreneurs as she exhibited innovation and the execution of good ideas, marketing over 300 creams and cosmetics in their familiar pink packages–Arden's favorite color. When Arden

died at the age of 88 in New York City, she was still the head and sole owner of her company. She left money to her sister Gladys, who oversaw the French operations of Elizabeth Arden, and to her niece Patricia Young, but the business was eventually sold to Eli Lilly and Company.

Where to learn more

Kanner, Bernice, "Beauty Makers," *Harper's Bazaar,* February 1991.

Lewis, Alfred Allan, *Miss Elizabeth Arden,* Coward, McCann, & Geoghegan, 1972.

Shuker, Nancy, *Elizabeth Arden: Cosmetics Entrepreneur,* Silver Burdett, 1989.

Hanan Ashrawi

Born 1946
Ramallah, Palestine (now the
Israeli-occupied West Bank)

Palestinian political activist and teacher

Became spokesperson for the Palestinian
cause in court of world opinion

"I am a descendant of the first Christians in the world, and Jesus Christ was born in my country, in my land. Bethlehem is a Palestinian town. So I will not accept this one-upmanship on Christianity. Nobody has the monopoly."

Hanan Ashrawi is a spokesperson and negotiator in the Palestinian cause for an independent state in the Holy Land. Educated in the United States, Ashrawi emerged as a persuasive spokesperson for her fellow Palestinians on the international stage as she advocated and represented the Palestinian position. Through her personal demeanor, intelligence, and command of the facts, she was a strong counterweight to the Western perception of Palestinians as terrorists.

Earns her doctorate

Ashrawi was born in 1946 in Ramallah, a town north of Jerusalem and now in the Israeli-occupied West Bank. Ashrawi is the youngest of five daughters of Daoud Mikhail and his wife. Mikhail was a physician in the Palestinian army and later a politician in Ramallah; Ashrawi credits him for instilling in her a commitment to the cause of Palestinian self-determination. "My father told us when we were young that

The significance of Palestine

Commonly called the Holy Land, Palestine is located on the eastern shore of the Mediterranean Sea and today comprises the modern states of Egypt, Israel, and Jordan. The boundaries vary but the land is always between the Mediterranean Sea and the Jordan River. In the Bible Palestine is referred to as Canaan before the invasion of Joshua, and the Hebrew name is Eretz Israel (land of Israel). Palestine is significant to three religions: For Jews it is the land promised to them by God; for Christians it is the birthplace of Jesus; and for Muslims Jerusalem is the place Muhammad ascended into heaven. During World War I (1914-1918) the British, aided by the Arabs, gained control of Palestine. Britain issued the Balfour Agreement in 1917 calling for a "national home" for Jews and a recognition of the rights of non-Jews. The agreement also allowed for the formation of individual states, which the Arabs believed to include Palestine, but the British later denied this interpretation. Following the first Arab-Jewish riots in 1920, the United Nations approved the Balfour Agreement and the British agreed to assist Jewish immigration within limits. Violence continued between Jews and Arabs until the persecution of Jews under the Nazi regime of Adolf Hitler influenced the United States to support an independent Jewish state. The British, unable to design a solution, turned the problem over to the United Nations in 1947. The result was formation of the state of Israel.

you have to be daring when you have right on your side," she has said. Attending the American University in Beirut, Lebanon, in the late 1960s, Ashrawi was involved in the General Union of Palestinian Students. She attended the 1969 international conference in Amman, Jordan, where she met Yasir Arafat, head of the Palestine Liberation Organization (PLO). After completing her master's degree in literature, Ashrawi taught at Bir Zeit University in the West Bank. In 1981 she enrolled at the University of Virginia in Charlottesville, earning a doctorate in English literature. She then returned to Bir Zeit University as a professor of English literature. Besides her scholarly work, Ashrawi has served as the school's dean of arts and belonged to the university's Human Rights Action Project. She and her husband, Emile Ashrawi, have two daughters, Amal and Zeina.

Protests Palestinian abuse

Ashrawi's beliefs turned radical after the massacre of Palestinian refugees in Beirut during Israel's invasion of Lebanon in 1982. "This has got to stop. Palestinians must not be an easy prey to everybody," said Ashrawi. Appearing on ABC's *Nightline* town meeting format, Ashrawi set herself apart by her superior performance. She appeared again and again on *Nightline,* being labeled "the Nightline Palestinian," as well as on the *MacNeil Lehrer NewsHour* on PBS, establishing herself as a reliable and articulate authority on Palestinian positions.

Madrid Conference

In 1991 the United States arranged a conference–informally called the Madrid Conference in reference to its being held in Madrid, Spain–to discuss the settlement of the Arab-Israeli conflict. According to the framework of the Camp David peace accord of 1979, separate negotiations could take place between Israel and its individual Arab neighbors. Since the PLO had appeared to side with Iraq during the Persian Gulf War, the Israelis wanted someone from the Palestinian delegation with no obvious ties to the PLO. They singled out Ashrawi. In behind-the-scenes negotiations with James Baker, the U.S. secretary of state, Ashrawi asserted that Palestinians had a right to select their own delegates without external interference. The American solution was to have Ashrawi and others form an advisory team at the conference separate from the official delegation accepted by Israel. The Israelis objected but then relented to this arrangement. About the arrangement, Yasir Arafat said, "No one can hide the sun with their fingers. Everyone knows that the Palestinians will represent the PLO." To the surprise of everyone at the Madrid conference, the Palestinians changed their position by expressing a willingness to accept a period of autonomy (greater freedom under Israeli rule) before becoming a fully independent state. Ashrawi was credited with creating this breakthrough, and again her reasonableness played well in the Western press.

Israel threatens arrest

Unhappy with Ashrawi's success in the international media, Israeli officials called for her arrest because she had broken the law that prevented meetings between the PLO and Palestinians living in Israel. It seems that prior to the Madrid Conference Ashrawi had traveled to Algiers in Africa to seek support from the Palestine National Council, which is part of the PLO. The ever-resourceful Ashrawi denounced the Israeli move, gained support from the Israeli Labour Party, and even convinced President George Bush to take her side. Confronted with these odds, the Israeli Justice Ministry backed down. Ashrawi intensified her media campaign, telling reporters, "They [the Israelis] are holding a whole people captive against their will. They are stealing these people's land and resources and freedoms and rights and the possibility of a future." The peace process made little headway in 1992 because of national elections in the United States and Israel. In 1993, however, a historic agreement between the PLO and Israel was reached.

In her recently published book, *This Side of Peace* (1995), which is part autobiography and part recent history, Ashrawi writes: "We cannot stand outside the course of history and say, 'I will pass judgment.' You're either an actor and a player, or you are acted upon and a victim. You have to always present constructive alternatives." No longer a spokesperson for the PLO, Ashrawi concentrates her energies on advocating Palestinian human rights. She still lives with her family in Ramallah on the West Bank.

Where to learn more

Ashrawi, Hanan, *This Side of Peace: A Personal Account,* Simon & Schuster, 1995.

Chicago Tribune, December 29, 1991.

Detroit Free Press, May 18, 1995, p. 1D.

New York Times, November 17, 1991, p. 3.

Time, May 25, 1992, p. 48.

Victor, Barbara, *A Voice of Reason: Hanan Ashrawi in the Middle East,* Harcourt Brace, 1994.

Nora Astorga

Born 1949
Managua, Nicaragua
Died February 14, 1988
Managua, Nicaragua

Nicaraguan civil servant

Member of Sandinista revolutionary group and Nicaraguan ambassador to the United Nations

Nora Astorga's involvement with Nicaragua's Sandinista government transformed her secretive revolutionary life to the life of a public figure as a United Nations delegate. A bilingual lawyer, Astorga became Nicaragua's chief delegate to the United Nations and also acted as her government's sole spokesperson, explaining its positions and policies to the rest of the world. Her revolutionary career started when she was involved in the violent death of one of the most hated generals in the Nicaraguan National Guard. It led her to commit to the financial and diplomatic rebuilding of her devastated country.

> "I didn't mind anymore about my life. I was willing to leave everything I had, including my kids. I told my companeros, I am ready to do more, something drastic."

Born into wealth

As the oldest child in a wealthy, land-owning Nicaraguan family, Astorga seemed headed toward the life of a typical aristocratic child. Astorga's grandfather had served as a defense minister in the government of Anastasio Somoza. Performing obligatory charity work at hospitals was Astorga's only childhood contact with poorer citizens of Nicaragua. However, seeing the poverty only convinced Astorga that she wanted to marry an aristocrat like herself and climb to the top of the social ladder. Astorga's father pushed her to excel academically and sent her to study at the Catholic University in Washington, D.C., in 1967. During her first two years in the United States, Astorga was not interested in her studies or in American culture. However, seeing the reaction of the African American community to the assassination of Dr. Martin Luther King, Jr., in 1968, left Astorga deeply moved. When her father demanded that she return to Nicaragua to study law, she realized that the Somoza regime had fostered the same type of class distinction in her own country. Having witnessed political unrest in the United States, Astorga returned to Nicaragua, fueled with the fire of revolution.

Becomes a revolutionary

While studying at the Jesuit-run Universidad Cantoamericana in Managua, Astorga became involved with the *Frente Sandinista,* a revolutionary group named after a guerrilla leader assassinated in 1934. Astorga wanted to go straight to guerrilla camp herself, and she was frustrated when the Sandinista leadership wanted her to work covertly and maintain her local status. Gradually she learned that every duty was important, and she began to run errands, pass messages, buy supplies, and provide refuge for people in her parents' houses. At the age of 22 she married fellow revolutionary Jorge Jenkins over her family's objections. The marriage lasted five years and produced two children, but Astorga would not abandon her work in the revolution to become a homemaker. She worked as a corporate lawyer in a Nicaraguan construction company and bought a house in an upper-class neighborhood of Managua. Her job enabled her to carry out her Sandinista assignments and gave her entry into influential circles within the Somoza regime. By the time she was 29, however, she was again discontented with the minor assignments given to her by the Sandinista revolution. Astorga wanted to do something dramatic and meaningful, and she was willing to risk everything to do it.

Involved in murder

The following year Astorga became involved in a conspiracy as dramatic as any for which she could have wished. She caught the eye of one of her company's clients, General Reynaldo Perez Vega. Vega was deputy commander of Nicaragua's National Guard and one of Somoza's most hated generals. When Astorga told the Sandinistas of Vega's interest, they decided to use her to set up the general. For more than a year she held out the possibility of a romantic relationship with Vega, despite the danger to her own children.

On March 8, 1978, Astorga called Vega's office to invite him to her home that evening. The general arrived with one bodyguard, then sent him away to get rum and cigarettes. When Vega least expected it, Astorga jumped out of hiding and murdered him. She claimed that the general's struggles resulted in "political justice" and not a planned kidnapping.

Leaving the general's body draped in a Sandinista flag, Astorga and her accomplices fled through the jungles to the Costa Rican border. There she trained as a combat soldier despite being pregnant. She took part in several battles and was regarded as a soldier equal to any man. Finally, in the last months of her pregnancy, she went to Costa Rica to do office work for the Sandinistas. When the Somoza regime fell in July 1979, she returned to Managua as a heroine of the revolution and an important member of the new government.

Joins new government

Astorga's first duty was to restore order to the army's finances, which had become tangled by more than 10 years of war. Then she was appointed head of the special tribunal called to hear the charges against members of Somoza's National Guard. Over 6,000 guardsmen were tried, and over 4,000 were given prison sentences of 30 years for the atrocities committed during the war. None were executed, however, for Astorga did not see the sense in a new government acting just like the old one.

Appointed U.N. ambassador

When her tribunal duties ceased, Astorga entered Nicaragua's foreign ministry. In 1983 she was named deputy foreign minister and began to make frequent trips abroad, representing her country's interests. The following year she was proposed as an ambassador to the United States. Employing a rarely used statute, the Reagan administration rejected her, saying that her guerrilla past made her undesirable. The United Nations could not block her nomination, however, and on March 11, 1986, she presented her credentials in New York to U.N. secretary general Javier Pérez de Cuellar. From the outset, the new Nicaraguan diplomat made her country's position clear. Criticizing the Reagan administration for providing aid to the contra rebels and working to overthrow the Sandinista government, Astorga called for peace. She asserted that peace could only come by cutting off U.S. aid immediately. Astorga quickly became the most visible ambassador within the United Nations by demanding that she be heard.

Leaves legacy of freedom

Shortly afterward, Astorga was diagnosed with breast cancer. Seven weeks after having a mastectomy, she returned to her U.N. post and worked a full schedule even while undergoing chemotherapy. In January 1988 she returned to Managua for more surgery. Although Astorga was expected to resume her U.N. duties, her condition quickly worsened, and she died on February 14, 1988, in Managua.

Where to learn more

Chicago Tribune, February 16, 1988.

New York Times, January 18, 1986; March 12, 1986; February 15, 1988.

Time, January 18, 1988.

Washington Post, February 15, 1988.

Charlotte Auerbach

Born May 14, 1899
Krefeld, Germany

German geneticist

Made important contributions
to the study of mutagenesis

Charlotte Auerbach is a German-born geneticist who revealed that chemicals can cause harm that can be passed on to the offspring of a species. She specialized in chemical mutagenesis (how chemicals cause genetic mutations, or changes, to the cells of living things). Her work on mutagens–particularly mustard gas–was performed initially on the fruit fly. Auerbach discovered the nature of genetic mutation, and she was highly decorated for her efforts.

Leaves Nazi Germany

Auerbach was born May 14, 1899, in Krefeld, Germany, to a scientifically inclined Jewish family. Her father was a chemist and an uncle was a physicist. Her grandfather, an anatomist, identified the interlacing of blood vessels and nerves in the human intestine, named the Auerbach's plexus. Charlotte Auerbach left Germany in 1933, because Adolf Hitler's Nazi government was enforcing repressive, anti-Jewish laws. She obtained her Ph.D. from the Institute of Animal Genetics in Edinburgh, Scotland, in 1935, and conducted most of her life's work there. She also conducted research in the United States and Japan.

In 1938 Auerbach worked with American geneticist Hermann Joseph Muller when he spent a year at the Institute of Animal Genetics. In 1927 Muller had shown how X-rays could mutate the genes of the fruit fly (its scientific name is Drosophila melanogaster). Genes, which carry the chemical code that determines inherited traits, are located on the chromosomes in an organism's cells. Mutations occur when chromosomes become changed or damaged. This happens spontaneously in nature and over time produces different traits in a species. However, when an organism is exposed to a mutagenic agent, the mutation rate increases dramatically, and many mutations have deadly consequences to the organism.

Discovers how mustard gas mutates genes

At the University of Edinburgh, Auerbach was asked to research the effects of mustard gas on Drosophila. Mustard gas, a chemical compound used as a weapon during World War I (1914-1918), was outlawed after the war. Because it seemed to have pharmacological effects similar to X-rays, scientists wondered if it might also have similar mutagenic effects. Auerbach's experiments produced results that were more dramatic than expected. Although other mutagens were being discovered in Germany, Switzerland, and the Soviet Union at about the same time, Auerbach's research had greater depth.

Her experiments on fruit flies revealed the relationship between chromosome breakage and gene mutation, and she discovered that chemical mutagens act more slowly on an organism than X-rays, yet produce devastating results. Auerbach also studied replication, or reproduction, of unstable genes in yeast (one-celled fungi) to find out how one-strand lesions in chromosomes are changed into two-strand mutations.

Discovers spontaneous mutations in bread mold

At the Oak Ridge (Tennessee) National Laboratory, Auerbach experimented on the bread mold Neurospora to show that spontaneous mutations occur even without chromosomes reproducing. She also analyzed mutagen specificity–that is, that certain mutagens act selectively on certain genes. Auerbach's successor, B. J. Kilbey, took her discoveries further by studying the metabolic and physiological changes that result when an organism's genes are mutated.

During the early 1950s the chemical properties of chromosomes, which carry the genetic code, was discovered to be DNA (deoxyribonucleic acid). Auerbach's research revealed that chemical mutagenesis is a multi-step process that starts with a chemical change in DNA.

As an expert in the field of chemical mutagens, Auerbach became involved in detecting and analyzing mutagens that act on the environment. She was a committee member and honorary president of the second International Congress on Environmental Mutagen Research, and she was a sponsor and adviser to the European Economic Community Program.

Honored for her achievements

Auerbach's work won her several honorary degrees from Leiden, Cambridge, and Dublin universities. She received the Keith Medal from the Royal Society of Edinburgh in 1947 and the Darwin Medal from the Royal Society of London in 1977. The University of Edinburgh awarded her a doctor of science degree in 1947 and in 1967 gave her a personal chair. Auerbach was elected to the Genetical Society of Japan in 1966 and the Danish Academy of Science in 1968, and she was appointed foreign associate of the U.S. National Academy of Sciences in 1970. She also won awards from the Environmental Mutagen Society of the United States in 1972 and from its European organization in 1974.

Where to learn more

Auerbach, Charlotte, *Genetics in the Atomic Age,* Oliver & Boyd, 1956.

Auerbach, Charlotte, *The Science of Genetics,* Harper, 1962.

Burns, George W. and Paul J. Bottino *The Science of Genetics,* 6th ed., Macmillan, 1988.

Aung San Suu Kyi

Born June 19, 1945
Rangoon, Burma
(now Yangon, Myanmar)

Myanmarese political activist

Winner of the Nobel Peace Prize for her work as the leader of Myanmar's pro-democracy movement

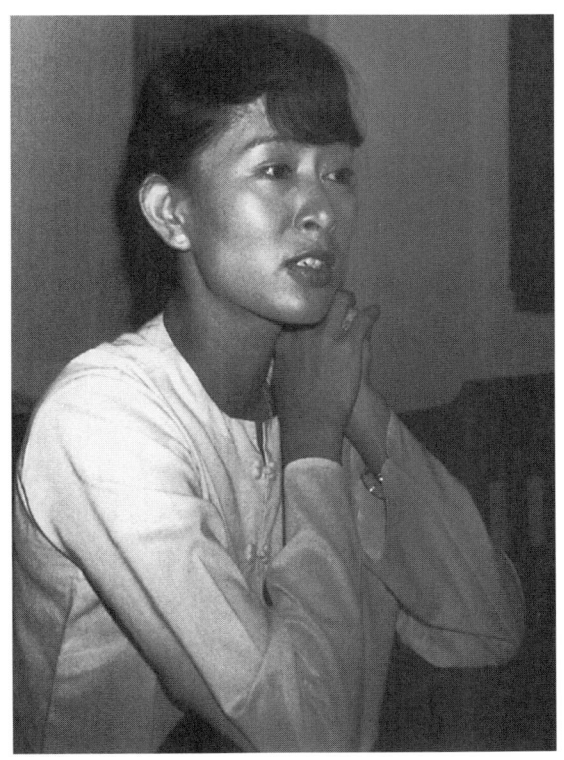

Winner of the 1991 Nobel Peace Prize, Aung San Suu Kyi was a political prisoner in Myanmar (the country was called Burma until 1990) from 1989 until 1995. Although she is the daughter of an important former leader of Burma, she spent most of her adult life in England, uninvolved in politics. She had not realized how bad conditions were in her homeland until she returned for a visit in 1988. Outraged by the actions of the government, she soon became active in reform efforts. During her imprisonment as the leader of Myanmar's pro-democracy movement she became a symbol of hope for a better future.

"Concepts such as truth, justice, and compassion cannot be dismissed as trite when these are often the only bulwarks which stand against ruthless power."

Born during a time of turmoil

Aung San Suu Kyi's father, U Aung San, was a beloved Burmese leader. Considered the founder of modern Burma, Aung San gained recognition during World War II (1939-1944), when he founded and led the Burma Independence

Army and later organized resistance against the invading Japanese. After the war, he headed the transitional government until 1947, when he was assassinated by political rivals. Aung San Suu Kyi was two years old at the time. For 15 years following Aung San's death, Burma was headed by his chief deputy, U Nu. During this time Burma became the richest nation in Southeast Asia. But in 1962 the government was toppled in a coup staged by U Ne Win, a brutal general. His leadership left the country in financial ruin and its people in fear for their lives.

Leaves Burma before coup

Aung San Suu Kyi lived in Burma until she was 17, when her mother was appointed Burma's ambassador to India. Later, she went to England, where she studied at Oxford University. There she married Michael Aris, a Tibet scholar at Oxford; they settled in Oxford and had two children. Because she had been away from Burma since 1960, Aung San Suu Kyi had witnessed none of the turmoil of Ne Win's authoritarian regime. But the more she learned about Burmese politics, the more she realized how much the memory of her father had kept alive the spirit of justice in Burma during all the years under a corrupt regime. In April 1988 Aung San Suu Kyi returned to Burma to take care of her dying mother. Late that summer, anti-government protests rocked Rangoon; at least 3,000 demonstrators were killed by Ne Win's troops. Horrified by what the government was doing to its own people, Aung San Suu Kyi felt compelled to speak out. At first, curious crowds came to hear her out of respect for her famous father. But soon they were coming by the thousands because of her impassioned call for democracy.

Organizes nonviolent resistance

Aung San Suu Kyi hoped that Burma could achieve democracy through nonviolent civil disobedience. She and other activists formed the National League for Democracy (NLD). Aung San Suu Kyi and the NLD kept up the pressure on the government throughout the rest of 1988, defying laws that prohibited gatherings of more than five people and public criticism of the armed forces. Aung San Suu Kyi in particular earned the admiration of the Burmese for her determination and courage as she faced troops who had been ordered to shoot her. General Ne Win's successor, General Saw Maung, promised that his government would step down after democratic elections scheduled for May 1990. Very few Myanmarese believed him. Aung San Suu Kyi continued to speak out against the government during 1989. In June her speeches took on an even bolder tone when she called on troops to overthrow the government. There was increased harassment of both Aung San Suu Kyi and other NLD leaders, many arrests, and widespread reports of torture and intimidation.

Imprisoned in her home

On July 20, 1989, after failing to silence her, military officials put Aung San Suu Kyi under house arrest in what had been her mother's home in Yangon (formerly Rangoon). She was forced to stay in her house without contact with Myanmar and the rest of the world, only infrequently being permitted to see her husband and children. Myanmar's leaders offered to release Aung San Suu Kyi if she agreed to leave the country quietly, but she refused to do so unless they released all political prisoners, honored the 1990 election results (in which the NLD won by a landslide), and allowed her to address the nation on television and radio. These conditions were denied by the military leaders. As Aung San Suu Kyi remained under house arrest, forbidden to see or even speak with anyone who was sympathetic to her cause, she became more popular than ever among Myanmarese. Her picture appeared everywhere, on illegal T-shirts, posters, and buttons, and her story was told in songs and poems. Because it was

dangerous to speak her name aloud, people referred to her as
"the Lady."

Awarded the Nobel Peace Prize

Aung San Suu Kyi's cause received more international
attention when she was awarded the 1991 Nobel Peace Prize
for her extraordinary acts of courage in the pursuit of democ-

racy. (Aung San Suu Kyi's husband and sons traveled to Norway and accepted the prize for her.) Human rights activists believed the prize might help keep Aung San Suu Kyi safe from execution. Others hoped the prize would encourage nations around the world to put more pressure on Myanmar to reform its political system. In light of worldwide recognition for Aung San Suu Kyi, her supporters remained hopeful that they would one day have freedom. Then nearly six years to the day after she was placed under house arrest, on July 10, 1995, Aung San Suu Kyi was freed. In an announcement that stunned the world, military leaders said her release was unconditional–she was free to come and go as she pleased, and she would not be forced to leave the country. On her first day of freedom Aung San Suu Kyi spoke to hundreds of ecstatic supporters, urging a spirit of compromise between the democracy movement and the military government.

Where to learn more

Aris, Michael, editor, *Freedom from Fear and Other Writings,* Penguin, 1991.

Maclean's, "A Fight for Rights," October 28, 1991, p. 84.

New York Times, October 15, 1991, p. A10; October 15, 1991, p. A11; October 20, 1991, p. 4E; November 24, 1991, p. 22; November 26, 1991, p. A21; December 11, 1991, p. A16; July 11, 1995, p. A1; July 12, 1995, p. A3; July 20, 1995, p. A11.

People, "The Wages of Courage," October 28, 1991, p. 129.

Time, July 31, 1989, p. 30; August 21, 1989, pp. 36-37; January 29, 1990, p. 57; October 28, 1991, p. 73.

Natalie Babbitt

Born July 28, 1932
Dayton, Ohio
American author and illustrator
Writes award-winning children's books

> *"You have to give writing your full attention, you have to like the revision process, and you have to like to be alone."*

Gifted storyteller and children's book writer Natalie Babbitt spins entertaining tales about characters facing challenges. Her originality, sense of humor, and courage have earned Babbitt a reputation as an important author of books for adults as well as children. She has won several awards, including the Christopher Award for Juvenile Fiction in 1976 and a National Book Award nomination in 1980.

Shows early interest in art

Natalie Babbitt owes her interest in literature to her mother, and she credits her sister for influencing her to become an illustrator. While Babbitt and her sister were growing up in Dayton, Ohio, their mother, Genevieve Moore, read children's books aloud to them. The two girls decided between them that Natalie would become an artist and her sister would be a writer. Impressed with Brazilian artist Luis de Vargas's airbrushed figures of glamorous women, which were popular during World War II, Babbitt copied the drawings with colored pencils. But the difference between Vargas's finished work and her own discouraged her. Sir John Tenniel's illustrations for the original publication of Lewis Carroll's *Alice in Wonderland* later inspired her to work with pen and ink, which eventually became her specialty.

Finds illustrating hard work

After taking a summer fashion illustration course at the Cleveland School of Art in Cleveland, Ohio, Babbitt realized she enjoyed creative drawing more than sketching dresses and sportswear. When she later took art classes at Smith College in Northampton, Massachusetts, she competed with other artists for the first time in her life, making her realize that success as an illustrator required more than creativity. In an autobiographical essay written years later, Babbitt explained: "It was an invaluable lesson, the best lesson I learned in four years of college: to wit, you have to work hard to do good work. I had always done what came easily, and what came easily had always been good enough. It was not good enough at Smith, and would never be good enough again."

Becomes wife and mother

After Babbitt married Samuel Babbitt in 1954, she worked and raised three children while her husband, an aspiring author, wrote a novel. When he discovered that the solitary writing life did not suit him, he went back to work as a college administrator. Babbitt's sister, pursuing her childhood decision, produced a comic novel for which Babbitt supplied illustrations, but she abandoned the project when an editor asked for substantial rewriting. Babbitt later wrote in an autobiographical essay that she learned a valuable lesson by observing what happened to her husband and sister when they tried to write novels. "But," she added, "it was years before I put any of it to good use."

Then Babbitt read *The Feminine Mystique,* the best-selling 1963 book by feminist leader **Betty Friedan** (see entry) which was critical of traditional women's roles. The book made her

Books by Natalie Babbitt

The Search for Delicious **(1969)** As 12-year-old Gaylen takes a poll of the kingdom to find the meaning of the word "delicious," unrest–as well as rumors of a mysterious mermaid named Ardis–grows.

Goody Hall **(1971)** When Midas Goody disappears in the English countryside, a young tutor sets out to find her.

The Devil's Storybook **(1974)** A trickster is fooled as often as he fools others.

Tuck Everlasting **(1975)** A family discovers a secret spring of youth, but finds that immortality causes problems.

realize that, although she had been a successful homemaker, she had neglected to develop her other talents. Discussions with other women who were making similar discoveries convinced her to pursue a second career as a professional illustrator. She drew the illustrations for her husband's book *The Forty-ninth Magician,* which was published in 1966 with the help of an editor at a New York publishing firm. After her husband became too busy to write stories, Babbitt illustrated her own books. The first two were picture books with stories in rhyming verse, *Dick Foote and the Shark* (1967) and *Phoebe's Revolt* (1968).

Begins writing career

The writing routine Babbitt follows is to start with a single image or word, then imagine the characters, whose personalities allow her to see what they will say naturally and how the story will progress. The finished product is often very different from her initial idea. For instance, she was thinking about the word "smuggler" when she started writing *Goody Hall,* but the book finally turned into a conversation with her mother, who had died when Babbitt was 24. When asked about this choice of story line, Babbitt recalled that her mother's death came at a time when she was "not yet mature enough to have figured [life] all out and discussed it with her. So I put it all into my story *Goody Hall* instead."

Creates unique characters

A Gothic mystery set in the English countryside, *Goody Hall* tells about the disappearance of Midas Goody; inspired to investigate Goody's disappearance, a young tutor who has an unusual mother encounters a Gypsy, a rich youngster, and an empty tomb. In Babbitt's next work, *The Devil's Storybook,* the title character is a trickster who is fooled as often as he tries to fool others, as when he gives the power of speech to a goat, then must put up with the talkative animal's constant complaining. In *Tuck Everlasting,* a family that discovers a secret spring of immortality finds that living forever without growing or changing is not a pleasant existence. According to a reviewer, Tuck's explanation of the role of death in the cycle of nature is "one of the most vivid and deeply felt passages in American children's literature."

Books reflect her own childhood

Looking back on her published work, Babbitt recognizes that her stories reflect many of her own childhood memories that have remained meaningful to her as an adult. Indeed, Babbitt's stories appeal to readers of all ages. As a *Horn Book* reviewer noted, "Babbitt's ... sense of humor, her wisdom and perspective on life, and her ability not to take herself too seri-ously–but to take what she writes and her audience very seri-ously–have shaped a magnificent body of work."

Where to learn more

Landsberg, Michele, "The Classic Shelf: *Tuck Everlasting* by Natalie Babbitt," *Ms.,* May 11, 1990, p. 74.

Meeker, Amy, "Natalie Babbitt: The Gifted Writer of Children's Books Has Returned to Her First Love–Illustrating Them" (interview), *Publishers Weekly,* February 21, 1994, p. 229.

Silvey, Anita, "A Rare Entity," *Horn Book,* March 1989, pp. 133-34.

Judith Baca

Born September 20, 1946
Los Angeles, California

Hispanic American artist,
muralist, and professor

Created the largest mural in the
world, The Great Wall of Los Angeles,
and cofounded the Social and
Public Art Resource Center

"If we cannot imagine peace as an active concept, how can we ever hope for it to happen?"

Judith Francisca Baca started her career as an artist by creating colorful murals (large wall paintings) to decorate the city of Los Angeles. Her work reflects her deep interest in social problems (particularly racism) and attracts international attention. Her best-known work is *The Great Wall of Los Angeles;* one-half mile in length, the outdoor mural is the largest in the world. Baca is also one of the founders of the Social and Public Art Resource Center in Venice, California, an organization that fosters the development of Hispanic artists.

Grew up with female role models

Baca was born September 20, 1946, in South Central Los Angeles. A second-generation Chicana (Mexican American woman), she was raised in a strong female household with her mother, grandmother, and two aunts, one of whom was mentally retarded. She did not know her musician father well, but she enjoyed a happy childhood. "It was a very strong, wonderful, matriarchal [mother as leader] household," she told an interviewer. "I was everybody's child. I had a wonderful playmate in my grown-up aunt who wasn't grown up in her head. It was like she was five, my age, only she was big."

When Baca was six years old, she moved with her mother to Pacoima, California. Since she had not yet learned English, she had a difficult time adjusting to school. Often feeling alone in the classroom, she became interested in art when one of her teachers allowed her to sit in a corner and paint while the rest of the students did their schoolwork.

After graduating from a Catholic high school in 1964, Baca attended California State University at Northridge. She earned a bachelor's degree in art in 1969, then returned to her high school to teach. She tried out her first cooperative art project that year, rounding up a group of ethnically diverse students to paint a mural at the school. It was "a method to force the group into cooperation," she recalls. It would come to be a method she would use many times in future projects.

Fired for war protests

During the late-1960s Baca joined the antiwar protests, marching–with several nuns who also taught at the high school–against the Vietnam War. School administrators did not approve of the antiwar activities, however, and fired all of the teachers involved. Out of work, Baca feared her teaching career was over.

Baca soon found a position in a special program for artists with the City of Los Angeles Cultural Affairs Division. Her new job required her to travel to schools and parks to teach art. In the areas where she worked, she noticed the art the teenagers had already created–graffiti, tattoos, and decorated cars. Baca realized they were using a visual language to express who they were and how they felt about their lives. Hoping to bring these teenagers together, she formed her own painting group, *Las Vistas Nuevas,* with 20 young people from neighborhood gangs and organizations. They worked together to paint Baca's first mural in Hollenbeck Park in Los Angeles.

Inspired by Mexican muralists

Because Baca admired the murals of great Mexican artists such as Diego Rivera and José Clemente Orozco, she traveled to Mexico to learn mural materials and techniques and to study the works of the Mexican masters. She has said: "I believe taking art to the people is a political act. I am a Mexican mural painter in the true sense, but I took it to the next level. To keep an art form living it has to grow and change."

When Baca returned to Los Angeles, she expanded her program into the Citywide Mural Project. Under her supervision, almost 250 murals were painted. Baca was the first in the city to assemble a multicultural group of young people to produce murals. Her most ambitious project during the 1970s was *The Great Wall,* which she painted on the walls of a San Fernando Valley drainage canal. The half-mile-long mural depicts the city's multiethnic history in pictures of important events from the Stone Age to the 1950s. Baca developed the concept, hired the workers, and helped raise the money for the project. Some of the teenagers who participated in the project did so to fulfill court sentences. *The Great Wall* took five summers, spread out over a period of nine years, to complete.

In 1976 Baca founded the Social and Public Art Resource Center (SPARC) in Venice, California. The nonprofit, multicultural art center brings together artists, community groups, and youth groups to create murals and preserve other public art. SPARC is an internationally recognized center that also keeps a library of 16,000 slides of public art from around the world.

Begins work on *World Wall*

In 1987 Baca began an even grander project, *World Wall: A Vision of the Future Without Fear,* which addresses issues of war, peace, cooperation, interdependence, and spiritual growth. Depicting spiritual and material changes that must occur on the planet before world harmony can be achieved, the portable mural is made of seven 10-by-30-foot panels painted by Baca. When four of the panels were completed in 1990, the mural was displayed in Finland and in countries of the former Soviet Union. The finished mural will include another seven panels to be painted by artists from the countries where it is exhibited.

Now a professor of art at the University of California at Irvine, Baca believes her art reflects her commitment to solving social problems, and she tries to inspire people to act on the positive possibilities in life. In her artist's statement for *World Wall,* she wrote that people have an easier time imagining a world caught in nuclear war than one that exists in perfect peace. She believes we must be able to imagine and picture peace in order to achieve it.

Where to learn more

Hispanic, May 1991, pp. 16-18.

Lippard, Lucy, *Mixed Blessings: Art for a Multicultural America,* Penguin Books, 1988.

Joan Baez

Born January 9, 1941
Staten Island, New York

Hispanic American singer, songwriter, and social activist

Folk singer, peace activist, and founder of Humanitas International

"I have been true to the principles of nonviolence, developing a stronger and stronger aversion to the ideologies of both the far right and the far left and ... [to] the suffering they continue to produce all over the world."

Often praised for her pure, beautiful voice, Joan Chandos Baez has earned fame as much for her political activism as for her singing. During the 1960s she made headlines by using her musical talent to campaign against America's involvement in the Vietnam War and against social injustice. She has continued her fight against social ills–not only in America but around the world–to the present day.

Influenced by Quaker upbringing

Baez was born January 9, 1941, in Staten Island, New York. From her Scottish mother, Joan Bridge, and her Mexican father, Albert Baez, she inherited a rich ethnic heritage. She also inherited their nonviolent Quaker religious beliefs, which would eventually inspire her own interests in peace and justice. Baez's father was a physicist who once turned down a high-paying job developing war weapons because of his moral standards.

Performing provides career direction

While growing up Baez was often taunted by other children because her skin was darker than theirs. In junior high school she felt isolated from her classmates. Her pacifist (antiwar) views further distanced her from her classmates, who held to the more militant, anticommunist beliefs of their parents. Loneliness led Baez to begin singing, which then proved to be a path to acceptance. She soon gained a reputation as a performer and made her first stage appearance in a school talent show. After she graduated from high school in 1958, she moved with her family to Boston, Massachusetts, where her father became a professor at Massachusetts Institute of Technology. Baez enrolled in Boston University, but her interest in music kept her away from her classes. At first she and a roommate sang duets in Boston-area coffeehouses, then she began performing solo and quickly attracted a large following of fans.

Withholds tax payments in protest of war

Baez began to act on her views about equal rights and pacifism. When she discovered that African Americans were not admitted to her concerts at white colleges in the South, she performed at black colleges. To protest the Vietnam War, Baez refused to pay the 60 percent of federal income taxes that she believed went to support the war effort. Around this time Baez became romantically involved with folk singer Bob Dylan and accompanied him on his first tour of England.

A career is launched

While singing at a Chicago nightclub in 1959, Baez caught the attention of Bob Gibson, a popular folk singer who asked her to appear with him at the first Newport (California) Folk/Jazz Festival. Her three-octave soprano voice and down-to-earth stage presence captivated the festival crowd of 13,000. She became a celebrity overnight. Many record companies–large and small–offered her recording contracts, and she signed her first contract with Vanguard, a small label known for its quality classical recordings. Her first solo album, titled *Joan Baez,* was released in 1960 and reached number three on the record charts. Baez moved to the Pacific coast in California, and as her popularity increased, she began to think about the world and her place in it. "I was in a position now to do something more with my life than just sing," she wrote in her autobiography. "I had the capacity to make lots and lots of money. I could reach lots and lots of people."

Baez performing at Giants Stadium in New Jersey.

Jailed for antiwar protests

In 1965 Baez founded the Institute for the Study of Non-violence (now called the Resource Center of Nonviolence) in Palo Alto, California. While her pacifism drew praise and support from some people, it angered others. U.S. Army bases worldwide banned her albums. In 1967 the Daughters of the American Revolution (DAR, a nonprofit organization of women that conducts historical, educational, and patriotic activities) refused Baez permission to perform at their Constitution Hall in Washington, D.C. When news of the refusal received sympathetic coverage in the press, Secretary of the Interior Morris Udall let Baez play an outdoor concert at the base of the Washington Monument. An estimated 30,000 people came to hear her sing. Several months later she was arrested and jailed for her acts against the Vietnam War draft. The following year Baez married David Harris, a leader in the draft resistance movement. In one of the highlights of her career, Baez performed at the famous Woodstock Music Festival, held near Bethel, New York, during the summer of 1969, which drew more than 500,000 people from all over America.

Tours North Vietnam

In 1971 Baez divorced Harris after having a son, Gabriel. She continued her musical career and her social and political activities. "The Night They Drove Old Dixie Down," a selection from her album *Blessed Are...,* became one of the most popular songs of 1972 and Baez's biggest commercial hit. She and a small group of friends toured North Vietnam in 1972 to witness the effects of the continuing war. On her return home, Baez edited 15 hours of tapes she had recorded during her trip and made them into *Where Are You Now, My Son?,* a personal plea for an end to the war. It was released as an album in 1973. That same year Baez organized an antiwar protest during which women and children joined hands around the Congress building in Washington, D.C. She has served on the national advisory board of the human rights organization Amnesty International, and she was instrumental in forming Amnesty West Coast in California. In 1979 she founded Humanitas International in Menlo Park, California, an organization that promotes human rights, disarmament, and nonviolence.

Performs at Live Aid concert to aid Ethiopian famine victims

Although Baez's popularity began to decline in the early 1980s, her career received a boost in 1985 when she opened the U.S. portion of Live Aid, the rock concert given by numerous performers and bands that raised money for famine victims in Ethiopia. The next year she participated with fellow musicians Sting, U2, and Peter Gabriel in the Conspiracy of Hope concert tour celebrating Amnesty International's 25th anniversary.

In 1987 Baez released her first album in eight years and published her autobiography, *And a Voice to Sing With.* Baez's pure and powerful voice has endured well throughout the years. Her 1993 release, *Play Me Backwards,* was nominated for a Grammy Award for best contemporary folk album. In 1995 Baez recorded a live album over four nights at the Bottom Line, a nightclub in Greenwich Village, New York, with singers Mary Chapin Carpenter, Kate and Anna McGarrigle, Janis Ian, Mary Black, and the Indigo Girls.

Continues peace effort

In 1988 Baez toured the Middle East to observe the conflicts between warring countries. In 1991 she announced plans to develop low-income housing in California. Two years later, in the cause of seeking a peaceful end to conflict, she toured the city of Sarajevo in war-torn Bosnia and Hercegovina (part of the former Yugoslavia).

Where to learn more

Baez, Joan, *Daybreak,* Dial Press, 1968.

Baez, Joan, *And a Voice to Sing With,* Summit Books, 1987.

Garza, Hedda, *Joan Baez,* Chelsea House, 1991.

Interview, April 1992, p. 98.

Rolling Stone, February 10, 1994, p. 43.

Oksana Baiul

Born November 16, 1977
Dnepropetrovsk, Ukraine
Ukrainian ice skater
1994 Olympic gold medalist in
singles freestyle ice skating

In her amazing young life, Oksana Baiul, overcame heart-breaking losses and setbacks, yet refused to quit. Virtually an unknown skater in 1992, this young figure skater made headlines a year later when she won the World Figure Skating Championship on her first try. She then went on to win the Gold Medal at the 1994 Winter Olympics in Lillehammer, Norway, overcoming a serious injury she had suffered during the pre-competition warm-ups.

Baiul was born November 16, 1977, in Dnepropetrovsk, the Russian-speaking Ukraine, which was part of the former Soviet Union and is about the size of Texas. When she was young, Baiul wanted to be a ballet dancer, but she needed to be thinner. To help her lose weight, her grandfather bought her ice skates. She turned out to be a natural figure skater who could jump and spin easily, and by the age of seven she was winning local competitions.

Baiul has lost several important people in her early life: Her father disappeared when she was two years old; the

"I like when people are watching. What's the reason for figure skating without spectators watching?"

grandmother who helped raise her died in 1987; and her grandfather died in 1988. Baiul's mother, Marina, who was a French teacher, died in 1991 of cancer when Baiul was 13. The two had been very close, and Baiul used skating to ease her pain and loss. After her mother died, for a short time Baiul slept on a cot at the skating rink, cooking her food on a hot plate.

Luck changes

Baiul suffered another loss when her coach of nine years, Stanislav Koretek, left the Ukraine in 1992 to work in Canada. Koretek's departure was very hard on Baiul, because she had lived with him after her mother had died, and he was the only adult left in her life. Before he left, Koretek asked Galina Zmievskaya to take over Baiul's training. Zmievskaya coached Viktor Petrenko, the 1992 men's figure skating Olympic gold medalist from the Ukraine and the husband to one of Zmievskaya's daughters. Baiul lived with Zmievskaya in Odessa, about 250 miles from Baiul's hometown. She shared a room with one of Zmievskaya's daughters. Petrenko, who is like a brother to Baiul, paid for her skates and outfits. Zmievskaya is a very strict coach and protective of her student, especially from questions about Baiul's painful past. Baiul appreciates all Zmievskaya has done for her and acknowledges, "She is like my mom."

Unknown skater

No one suspected that Baiul would become a world-champion skater. In 1991 she finished twelfth in the Soviet Union National Figure Skating Championships. She improved under Zmievskaya's coaching and won the 1993 Ukrainian National Figure Skating Championship, which gave her the right to compete in the European Figure Skating Championships. To everyone's surprise, Baiul finished second in the 1993 European championships held in Helsinki, Finland, even though she had competed only twice outside of her home country.

Major upset

Baiul came as a virtual unknown to the 1993 World Figure Skating Championships in Prague, Czechoslovakia. Since skaters usually are not successful in their first world championship competition, Baiul was not expected to do well. In fact, Baiul had never competed in the World Junior Figure Skating Championships. Nancy Kerrigan, representing the United States, finished first in the short, or technical, program, but Baiul placed second. In the long, or free skating, program, Kerrigan had problems with her jumps and fell out of contention. Baiul made the most of this chance. When the final scores were totaled, Baiul won the championship, edging out Surya Bonaly of France–who had defeated her for the European title. At 15 Baiul became the youngest woman to win the world championship since the legendary Sonja Henie of Norway won at age 14 in 1927. Baiul was also the first woman from one of the countries of the former Soviet Union to win the single's world championship. After she won, Baiul wept. "My tears are God's kisses from my mother," she explained after her victory.

Crowd pleaser

Baiul's success was due in part to her ability to entertain the crowd as well as the figure skating judges. She skates with a dazzling smile on her face, puts energy into her performances, and waits after her name is announced before skating to the center of the ice to begin her program. She has a reason for this delay: "I listen to my skates. When they can start, they go to the start." Baiul is not a skater of strength, although she can complete all of the difficult triple jumps. However, she skates extremely well to her music and touches the hearts of audiences and judges with her grace and style. After her success in the world championships, Baiul began to train with her idol, three-time U.S. women's figure skating champion Jill Trenery, whom Baiul admires for her beauty on the ice. Baiul began her tour of the United States–the first time she had ever been in America–and she enjoyed staying in hotels, eating in restaurants, and performing before her new fans.

Baiul giving her gold
medal performance during
the 1994 Winter
Olympics.

No pressure

After the tour, Baiul began training for the Olympics and returned to school where she was in the 11th grade. She was one of the favorites going into the 1994 Winter Olympics in Lillehammer, Norway, despite finishing second to Bonaly in the 1994 European championships. "It is not important to be always first," she said after the European competition. She even claimed that training for the Olympics did not put her under pressure: "I don't feel any pressure. I like to compete and show my programs and see how the people will react."

Bad luck returns

There was a sense of high drama over the women's figure skating, because one of the U.S. competitors, Nancy Kerrigan, had been injured in the knee by associates of her teammate, Tonya Harding. Knocked out of the U.S. Figure Skating Championships, Kerrigan worked her way back into shape and won the technical program as the Olympic competition began. Baiul finished second, and Bonaly, third. A slight stumble on one of her jumps cost Baiul the lead, but the scoring was so close that the long program would decide the competition. Then Baiul collided with another skater during practice the day before the long program, injuring her back and gashing her leg. No one knew if Baiul would be able to skate in the long program.

Wins Olympic Gold Medal

Both Baiul and Kerrigan skated in the long program, with only a slight stumble by Baiul separating the two skaters. In one of the closest finishes in Olympic figure skating history, Baiul won the Gold Medal when five of the nine judges gave her a higher score than Kerrigan on her long program.

The difference between the two had less to do with skating and more to do with style. "[Baiul] gives emotion to the referees and to the public," said Philippe Candeloro of France, the men's bronze medalist. "Oksana ... plays on a stage. The judges are people, and they appreciate the attention she gives them. She makes them the most important part of her performance," said American Paul Wylie, the 1992 Olympic men's silver medalist. Baiul broke down in tears when she won. She became the youngest Olympic figure skating champion since Henie won in 1928. Baiul's victory was saddened when Petrenko, a favorite for the men's Gold Medal, fell during his short program and finished fourth. Still bothered by her injuries, Baiul decided not to compete in the 1994 world championships.

Where to learn more

Detroit Free Press, February 24, 1994.

People, December 6, 1993.

Sporting News, February 14, 1994; March 7, 1994.

Sports Illustrated, March 22, 1993; February 7, 1994.

Sports Illustrated for Kids, February 1994.

Ella Baker

Born December 13, 1903
Norfolk, Virginia

Died December 13, 1986
New York, New York

African American civil rights activist

Civil rights worker and first
female president of an NAACP chapter

A fervent civil rights worker, Ella Baker organized and participated in the watershed events to wrest the same rights for African Americans that white Americans enjoyed. She led chapters of the National Association for the Advancement of Colored People (NAACP) and was the first woman ever to be president of one of its chapters. She co-founded the Southern Christian Leadership Conference (SCLC) and directed it for two years. She also co-founded the Student Nonviolent Coordinating Committee (SNCC, pronounced "snick") and the Mississippi Freedom Democratic Party (MFDP). All of these groups achieved substantial gains in the area of civil rights during her watch.

"I don't claim to have a corner on an answer, but I believe that the struggle is eternal. Somebody else carries on."

Committed to social causes

Baker was born in Norfolk, Virginia, in 1903, to Blake and Georgianna Baker. Her father was a ferryboat waiter, and her mother was a teacher. Baker grew up in North Carolina in a small, rural community. In 1927 she graduated from Shaw University in Raleigh, North Carolina, at the top of her class. At that time teaching was the only profession open to educated southern African American women, but Baker preferred an occupation as a medical missionary, a sociologist, or a social worker. She moved to New York City to find work, at first waitressing, then doing factory work. She also wrote for newspapers, first an American West Indian newspaper, then the *Negro National News*.

Forms cooperative grocery stores

Living in New York City during the Great Depression, a period of severe economic crisis in the 1930s, Baker saw many people out of work and struggling to meet basic needs. In 1932 she started the Young Negroes' Cooperative League with George Schuyler, a leading black newspaper writer. They formed groups called cooperatives, which were different from regular grocery stores because they were owned by the customers. Baker became so adept at buying quality goods for less money that the Works Progress Administration (WPA), a government-sponsored jobs program, hired her to teach buying classes.

First woman to hold NAACP chapter president office

By 1940 Baker was working as a field organizer for the NAACP, making every effort to register new African American voters and fighting segregation in the South. In 1942 she became nationwide director of branches for the NAACP. Four years later she resigned the post, because she had taken on the responsibility of raising her eight-year-old niece, Jackie Brockington. When Jackie turned 16, Baker returned to the NAACP, this time as president of the New York City branch, the first woman ever to achieve that status within the NAACP. She became involved in the struggle to integrate New York City's public schools.

Joins bus boycott

In 1955 thousands of African Americans in Montgomery, Alabama, stopped riding public buses for 381 days. This action, known as the Montgomery bus boycott, was organized by the Montgomery Improvement Association (MIA) in response to the arrest of **Rosa Parks** (see entry), who refused the bus driver's order that she give her seat to a white passenger. Baker went to Alabama to advise MIA leaders, and with other civil rights activists founded a group called In Friendship, which raised money for the boycott. Ultimately, the protest was successful: In 1956 the U.S. Supreme Court ruled that the bus company and the city of Montgomery had to allow black passengers to sit wherever they wished.

In 1957 Baker and the other boycott leaders met with southern African American ministers and formed the Southern Christian Leadership Conference (SCLC) to help church-based movements work together. Baker directed the SCLC from 1958 through 1960 with the official title of acting director, the title being a concession to the board of directors who preferred that the job be given to a minister.

They called her "Fundi"

Those who knew Baker called her "Fundi," a Swahili word for a person who masters a craft with the help of his or her community, practices it, then teaches it to the next generation. Baker's craft was organizing people to work together for social change. In 1981 gospel singer/historian Bernice Johnson Reagon wrote a song about Baker, "Ella's Song," which celebrates her role as "Fundi" to the American civil rights movement: "That which touches me most is that I had the chance to work with people/Passing on to others that which was passed on to me."

Known as godmother of the SNCC

Meanwhile, throughout the South, students were holding sit-in demonstrations to protest discrimination against African Americans at lunch counters, movie theaters, libraries, courthouses, and full-service restaurants. Baker and some of the student leaders thought these protests could be even more effective if the various student groups worked together. In 1960 Baker called the student leaders together, which led to the formation of the Student Nonviolent Coordinating Committee (SNCC). SNCC led voter registration drives in the

*Baker (left) speaking at a **Jeannette Rankin** (see entry) news conference in 1968, on behalf of the Southern Conference Educational Fund.*

rural South. African Americans who tried to vote often risked their lives, because whites were intent on keeping blacks from voting.

In 1964 SNCC organized the Mississippi Freedom Democratic Party (MFDP) to give African American Democrats in Mississippi an alternative to the regular Democratic party, which they felt excluded them. That year the MFDP held a convention in Jackson, Mississippi, at which Baker was the keynote speaker. She then went to Washington, D.C., to open the party's national office. In the ensuing years many MFDP candidates were elected to local, state, and eventually national offices. MFDP efforts have been credited with winning passage of the Voting Rights Act of 1965, which made it illegal to deny any adult U.S. citizen the right to vote.

Soon after the Voting Rights Act was passed, Baker moved back to Harlem, where she continued to advise SNCC, SCLC, and MFDP. She also devoted her energies to community organizations and international human rights movements, particularly the African National Congress, the Puerto Rican Solidarity Committee, and liberation groups in Zimbabwe, South Africa. In 1981 she was the subject of the documentary *Fundi: The Story of Ella Baker.* Baker died on December 13, 1986, her 83rd birthday.

Where to learn more

Branch, Taylor, *Parting the Waters: America in the King Years, 1954-1963,* Simon & Schuster, 1988.

Cantarow, Ellen, and others, *Moving the Mountain: Women Working for Social Change,* Feminist Press, 1980.

Dallard, Shyrlee, *Ella Baker: A Leader Behind the Scenes,* Silver Burdett Press, 1990.

The Eyes on the Prize Civil Rights Reader, Penguin, 1991.

Powledge, Fred, *Free At Last? The Civil Rights Movement and the People Who Made It,* Little, Brown, 1991.

Josephine Baker

Born June 3, 1906
St. Louis, Missouri
Died April 12, 1975
Paris, France

American/French performer

Introduced "hot jazz" to Paris; named Chevalier of the French Legion of Honor for intelligence gathering during World War II

"I don't want to be without Paris. It's my country. Understand? I have to be worthy of Paris. I want to become an artist."

Josephine Baker is the spirited, glamorous entertainer who introduced "hot jazz" to Paris. The toast of France, she was known for her extravagant performances and exotic costumes. The feather skirt she wore at the Folies-Bergère, a Paris music hall, created a sensation, as did the leopard she led along Paris streets. Baker spied for the French Resistance during World War II (1939-1945), and the French Government recognized her by awarding her the Rosette of the Resistance and naming her a Chevalier of the French Legion of Honor.

Gets her start in vaudeville

Baker was born Josephine Carson on June 3, 1906, in St. Louis, Missouri, the first child of Eddie Carson, a drummer, and Carrie McDonald. Before Baker was a year old her father had left the family, and by the time she was eight she was working as a live-in housekeeper. After a failed marriage to Willie Wells, she joined a group of street performers called the Jones Family Band. Her first appearance on stage was at the Booker T. Washington Theater, a black vaudeville house in St. Louis. The Dixie Steppers, an all-black traveling troupe, was also performing at the theater, and soon Baker became a dresser for the Steppers' star performer. While touring with the Dixie Steppers in 1920–when she was only 14–she married Willie Baker, a Pullman porter, and changed her name to Josephine Baker.

Appears in first successful show

In 1921 Baker had a chance to appear in *Shuffle Along,* a show by the famous black composers Noble Sissle and Eubie Blake. *Shuffle Along* was playing in Philadelphia, then would be going on to play on Broadway in New York City. Baker was too young to join the company, but she became so obsessed with performing in *Shuffle Along* that she left her husband and went to New York City. She took a job as a dresser with the show and learned all the songs and dances. When one of the chorus girls became ill, Baker took the dancer's place on stage. Audiences loved her, and she became a box office draw. She traveled with the road company until *Shuffle Along* closed in 1924.

Recruited for La Revue Nègre

Baker then joined the chorus at the Plantation Club in New York City's Harlem district. One night Caroline Dudley, a wealthy black producer, visited the club looking to recruit singer Ethel Waters for *La Revue Nègre,* a black revue Dudley wanted to take to Paris. When Waters declined, Dudley took Baker instead. *La Revue Nègre* opened in Paris at the Théâtre des Champs Élysées to an enthusiastic reception. Deciding that the tap dancing and blues singing needed to be more exotic, the theater owners added *Danse Sauvage*–the Savage Dance–a "hot jazz" routine that featured Baker with a male partner, Joe Alex. Wearing only a feather skirt, Baker became an overnight sensation. Shortly after *La Revue Nègre* opened, she was asked to join the Folies-Bergère, the premier Paris music hall, for its new show in April 1926. In the meantime, she went with *La Revue Nègre* to Germany, where German intellectuals and artists proclaimed her a genius.

Inspires dolls, perfumes, and Bakerfix hair products

When Baker joined the Folies-Bergère, she starred in a production called *La Folie du Jour,* another "exotic" tableau in which she wore a skirt of plush bananas. By late 1926 the dancer was the subject of a merchandising boom. People bought "Josephine" dolls and perfume. Women used a product called Bakerfix to slick down their hair like Baker's. Baker opened her own club–Chez Josephine–although it closed within a year, and she recorded several songs for the Odeon recording company. Having learned to speak French fluently, Baker performed in a French-language motion picture called *La Sirène des Tropiques* in 1927, then toured Europe and Argentina.

Baker and her leopard create sensation on streets of Paris

In 1930 the "new" Josephine Baker opened at the Casino de Paris in a revue called *Paris qui Remue.* When the producer bought her a leopard named Chiquita, Baker and Chiquita became an instant sensation in fashionable Parisian circles. She also starred in two films in the 1930s, *Zou-Zou* and *Princess Tam-Tam,* and in the fall of 1934 she was featured in *La Creole,* an operetta by 19th-century French composer Jacques Offenbach.

In 1935 Baker decided to return to America and re-create the sensation she made in Paris with the Ziegfeld Follies of 1936. After the show received poor reviews, Baker opened a club in New York, but it closed shortly thereafter. Deciding to make a clean break with her past, she divorced Willie Baker and married Jean Lion, a French sugar broker. Through this brief marriage she became a French citizen.

Selected films featuring Josephine Baker

Zou Zou (**1934**) This lavish musical drama tells the story of a laundress who fills in for the leading lady on the opening night of a show and becomes a hit. In French with English subtitles.

Princess Tam Tam (**1935**) A beautiful native African woman is "westernized" by a handsome writer and then introduced to high society as an exotic princess. In French with English subtitles.

Spies on behalf of French Resistance

In September 1939, when France declared war on Germany, Baker was recruited by the Deuxième Bureau, the French military intelligence. She spent the years during World War II obtaining information for the bureau as an "honorable correspondent." After the German occupation of France, Baker left Les Milandes, the French country estate she had bought in 1936, and moved to Morocco. In 1942 she toured North Africa, performing for French, British, and American soldiers. In the Middle East she did benefit performances for the French resistance, an underground movement that worked against the German occupation of France. For her efforts on behalf of France, Baker was made a lieutenant in the Women's Auxiliary of the French Air Force. After Paris was liberated in August 1944, Baker returned to France. In 1946 she was awarded the Rosette de la Resistance and was made a chevalier of the Legion of Honor.

Adopts 12 children; calls them her "Rainbow Tribe"

In 1947 Baker married Jo Bouillon, a French orchestra leader. During a tour of the United States, Baker insisted on a nondiscrimination clause in her contracts and integrated audi-

ences at her performances. The National Association for the Advancement of Colored People (NAACP) declared May 20, 1951, Josephine Baker Day in honor of her efforts against racism. Then she adopted children of different ethnic backgrounds whom she raised in an atmosphere of harmony at Les Milandes, which she and Bouillon had refurbished after the war. She called the group her "Rainbow Tribe." By 1962 she had adopted twelve children–ten boys and two girls–but by February 1964 Les Milandes was in serious financial trouble. For four years Baker managed to keep the estate from being seized by the French government, but she was finally evicted in 1968. Her predicament attracted the attention of Princess Grace of Monaco, who arranged for Baker and her children to live in a villa in Roquebrune, near Monte Carlo.

Baker's final show, called *Josephine,* told her life story in a series of scenes. It opened in Paris April 8, 1975, to favorable reviews, but four days later Baker had a stroke in her sleep and died. Twenty thousand people attended her funeral at the church of the Madeleine in Paris, and the ceremony was broadcast on French national television.

Where to learn more

Baker, Jean-Claude, *The Hungry Heart,* Random House, 1993.

Baker, Josephine and Jo Bouillon, *Josephine,* translated by Mariana Fitzpatrick, Harper & Row, 1977.

Haney, Lynn, *Naked at the Feast: A Biography of Josephine Baker,* Dodd, Mead, 1981.

Rose, Phyllis, *Jazz Cleopatra: Josephine Baker in Her Time,* Doubleday, 1989.

Sara Josephine Baker

Born November 15, 1873
Poughkeepsie, New York
Died February 22, 1945
New York, New York

American physician

Revolutionized pediatric health care in the United States

> *"I had a sincere conviction that they [slum babies] would all be better off dead than so degradingly alive.... Here was a great waste. My problem was how to prevent it."*

Sara Josephine Baker headed the child hygiene division of the Department of Health and reduced New York City's infant mortality rate to the lowest of all major cities worldwide. She was the first woman in the United States to hold an executive position in a health department and the first woman to receive a doctorate in public health. Baker innovated health reform policies and made preventive medicine and health education the responsibility of government. She also represented the United States on the health committee of the League of Nations in the early 1920s.

Born November 15, 1873, in Poughkeepsie, New York, Baker was the daughter of affluent parents. Her father, Orlando Daniel Mosser Baker, was a lawyer and a Quaker, and her mother was one of the first women to attend Vassar College. Baker's Aunt Abby, also a Quaker, encouraged the young girl. She grew up in an environment that accepted women as equals, an attribute of the family's Quaker background.

Becomes a doctor

When Baker was 16 years old, her father and brother died from typhoid fever (a bacterial disease that spreads in contaminated food or water). Brokenhearted, she abandoned plans to attend Vassar and went directly to New York Women's Medical College to become a doctor. In 1898 Baker graduated second in her class. She served her internship at the New England Hospital for Women and Children, an outpatient clinic in one of the worst slums in Boston, Massachusetts. Later she moved to New York City with her roommate and set up a joint practice near Central Park West. At the same time Baker was a medical inspector for the New York City Department of Health, examining sick children in schools and trying to control the spread of contagious disease.

Becomes first woman health official

In 1902 Baker took a job searching for sick infants in Hell's Kitchen. Located near the docks of Manhattan's West Side, Hell's Kitchen was a slum where 1,500 children a week died of dysentery (a disease that causes severe diarrhea and dehydration). In 1908 the Department of Health created the child hygiene division and installed Baker as its director, making her the first woman in the United States to hold an executive position in any health department. There she shaped policies for innovative health reform and made preventive medicine and health education a government obligation. As Baker's program saved the lives of countless infants, she revolutionized pediatric health care in the United States and in other nations as well.

Shapes nation's public health system

One of Baker's projects was the "milk station." Established throughout the city, nurses examined babies, dispensed milk, and scheduled checkups. In 1911, 15 milk stations prevented more than 1,000 deaths, and the next year 40 more stations were opened. In another project, Baker trained and licensed midwives (persons who assist women in childbirth).

Midwifery was a common practice in Europe, and many immigrant women were reluctant to allow their babies to be delivered by male doctors in hospitals. Midwives were often untrained, however, and infant death rates were high. Baker founded a mandatory licensing program that was so successful that infection rates for home deliveries were lower than hospital rates.

Baker then started the Little Mothers League. Young girls often cared for younger siblings while their mothers worked. The Little Mothers League trained the girls in the feeding, exercising, dressing, and general care of infants. Baker is also credited with originating the foster care system, which significantly reduced infant mortality. It placed orphaned babies in homes instead of institutions. During Baker's direction, death rates fell from one-half to one-third of infants born in a year. She also introduced the idea of pre-natal care to prevent infant mortality during and following childbirth. Baker set up a school inspection system, and the health department's recordkeeping procedures she streamlined were adopted nationwide. She opened specialized clinics and began sending public health nurses out to train parents. In 1912 she established the Federal Children's Bureau and made plans to create a division of child hygiene in every state.

NYU admits women

Baker also induced New York University (NYU) Medical School to drop its policy against admitting women to their school. In 1915 NYU officials asked Baker to teach child hygiene for a class in their doctor of public health degree program. Baker, who did not have a degree in this field herself, offered to teach in return for the opportunity to earn the diploma. Dean William Park informed her that the medical school did not admit women, so Baker refused to teach. For a year Park searched for another instructor, and when he could not find one, he admitted Baker and other women to the program. She taught at NYU for 15 years.

Women's suffrage was another issue to which Baker devoted her energy. She and five other women founded the

College Equal Suffrage League, an organization that campaigned for women's voting rights. Baker marched in the first annual Fifth Avenue suffrage parade.

Appointed League of Nations representative

From 1922 to 1924 Baker served as U.S. representative to the League of Nations health committee, and she was consulting director in maternity and child hygiene of the U.S. Children's Bureau. After retirement she sat on more than 25 committees devoted to improving children's health care. She also served a term as president of the American Medical Women's Association. Baker died of cancer on February 22, 1945, in New York City. Her preventive health policies saved hundreds of thousands of babies and reduced the infant mortality rate significantly: in 1907 one baby died for every six babies born; by 1943, because of Baker's effective policies, only one baby died for every twenty babies born.

Where to learn more

James, Edward T., editor, *Notable American Women: A Biographical Dictionary,* volume I, Belknap Press, 1975.

Morantz, Regina Markell, Cynthia Stodola Pomerleau, and Carol Fenichel, editors, *In Her Own Words: Oral Histories of Women Physicians,* Yale University Press, 1982, p. 30.

Morantz-Sanchez, Regina Markell, *Sympathy and Science: Women Physicians in American Medicine,* Oxford University Press, 1985.

Peavy, Linda and Ursula Smith, *Women Who Changed Things,* Charles Scribner's Sons, 1983, p. 122.

Daisy Bates

Born 1920
Huttig, Arkansas

African American journalist
and civil rights activist

Led school integration effort
in Little Rock, Arkansas

"Instinctively I threw myself to the floor. I was covered with shattered glass. L.C. rushed into the room. He bent over me as I lay on the floor. 'Are you hurt? Are you hurt?' he cried. 'I don't think so'."

Daisy Bates assured herself a place in the history books with her courageous efforts to integrate Central High School in Little Rock, Arkansas, during the late 1950s. Despite threats, criminal charges, and mob violence, Bates led nine black children through a crowd of angry white citizens so they could attend school. As the leader of the Arkansas conference of the National Association for the Advancement of Colored People (NAACP), Bates was in the forefront of the civil rights movement. "She was a good infighter, persistent, intelligent, unintimidated–a woman who made a choice of this career fully aware of its dangers to her person and also its rewards in the prestige and service of her people," Elizabeth Huckaby, vice-principal of Central, once said of Bates.

Starts innovative newspaper

Bates was born in 1920 in Huttig, a small town in southeast Arkansas. Raised by adoptive parents, Orlee and Susie

Smith, she never knew her birth parents. She attended a segregated public school in Huttig, where the students used textbooks that were discarded from the white school. When she was 15 she met Lucius Christopher Bates, an insurance salesman and close friend of her father. In 1941 the two married and settled in Little Rock. They used their savings to lease the *Arkansas State Press,* and within the first few months they increased circulation to 10,000. The *Arkansas State Press* was a successful paper that strived for better social and economic conditions for blacks throughout the state. It exposed police brutality in Little Rock, eventually bringing about changes. For instance, black police officers were hired to patrol black neighborhoods, improving race relations in the community.

Becomes civil rights activist

When the U.S. Supreme Court declared segregation in public schools unconstitutional in May 1954, the superintendent of Little Rock school system announced that the school board would seek gradual integration. The state and local NAACP branches decided to challenge the board's policy. As president of the state conference of NAACP branches since 1952, Bates was placed at the center of national and international attention for months. Several hundred African American children were polled by school officials to see if they were eligible for admission to Central High School. Eighty were chosen, and then when additional factors were considered–scholastic achievement and emotional stability– officials announced that only 17 could apply. Of those 17 only nine agreed to attend an integrated school. Bates promised to protect these children, despite threats of violence and economic retaliation.

On May 31, 1955, the Supreme Court announced that public school integration must proceed "with all deliberate speed." During the 1955-56 and 1956-57 school years, the NAACP leadership placed pressure on the Little Rock school board to implement its announced integration program. In February 1956 NAACP lawyers filed suit in federal court to gain the admittance of the children to white public schools at midsemester. Federal Judge John Miller decided to go along with Little Rock school board's timetable for integration, but ruled that integration would have to begin on September 4, 1957.

Violence erupts

On August 22, 1957, a rock was thrown through the front window of Bates's home. The nine students chosen to attend Central High School had some misgivings about putting themselves in a potentially dangerous situation, but they and their parents had faith in Bates. She had successfully challenged white school authorities with the legal backing of the NAACP. On August 29, 1957, Judge Murray O. Reed halted the integration of Central High School due to rumors that white and black children were forming gangs and that some of them carrying knives and guns. NAACP lawyers successfully appealed the decision, and on September 2, 1957, the Arkansas National Guard arrived at Central High School to prevent an outbreak of violence. The school board asked the black students not to try to enroll at any white school.

Rumors circulated that a white mob was forming around the high school and other areas of the city. Bates contacted members of the Interracial Ministerial Alliance and asked that ministers accompany the students to the school. Some ministers agreed, planning to walk with the children the next morning. Bates called the parents of all the children–except for the parents of Elizabeth Eckford, since the Eckfords did not have a phone. On September 23, after Bates had the children gather outside her home, she quietly escorted them into the school. That morning Eckford went to Central High School by herself, and hundreds of white students and citizens taunted and jeered her, with reporters and photographers from around the world witnessing the event. She displayed dignity under pressure and became a source of inspiration to other blacks.

Federal involvement

The attack on Eckford set off a round of mob violence in the city that lasted 17 days. The children left the school

through a delivery door and stayed at home the next day. Meanwhile, President Dwight D. Eisenhower federalized all units of the Arkansas National Guard and ordered the Secretary of Defense Charles Wilson to enforce the integration laws. Wilson ordered 1,000 paratroopers to the area, and President Eisenhower went on television to announce that the troops would enforce federal law in Little Rock. On September 25 the children again met at Bates's home, and she escorted them to school under federal troop supervision. The paratroopers remained at Central High School until September 30, then returned to their base, 12 miles away from the city. The federalized Arkansas National Guard remained on patrol at the school.

Achieves her goal

On October 31 the Little Rock city council ordered the police chief to arrest Bates, Crenshaw, and any other NAACP officials he could find. They were in violation of the new statute that required organizations to supply information about membership, contributors, and expenditures. Editorials across the country decried Bates's arrest, and the court eventually fined her only $100. Despite the best efforts of white racists, Bates was able to guide the nine students through the school year. For the rest of the 1950s and early 1960s she turned her attention toward voter education and registration programs. Although slowed by illness, she still sits on numerous boards in community organizations, and the press and politicians still seek her comments on issues facing the black community.

Where to learn more

Bates, Daisy, *The Long Shadow of Little Rock,* David McKay Co., 1962.

Freyer, Tony, *The Little Rock Crisis: A Constitutional Interpretation,* Greenwood Press, 1984.

Williams, Juan, *Eyes of the Prize: America's Civil Rights Years, 1954-1965,* Penguin Books, 1987,

Kathleen Battle

Born August 13, 1948
Portsmouth, Ohio
African American opera singer
Internationally known soprano

Kathleen Battle is one of the premier opera singers in the world who is noted for her roles in the coloratura (elaborate embellishment in vocal music) and soubrette (comic opera roles) repertoires. After debuting with the Michigan Opera Theater in 1976, Battle has appeared in major festivals, toured and recorded extensively, and appeared on Grammy Awards shows. She has also performed with major orchestras including the New York Philharmonic, Cleveland Orchestra, and Los Angeles Philharmonic.

Learned to sing from her father

Battle, the youngest of seven children, was born on August 13, 1948, in Portsmouth, Ohio, to a steelworker. She learned to sing from her father, who sang in a gospel quartet, and her sister taught her to read music. By looking over other people's shoulders she learned how to play the piano.

"I learned to sing listening to my father. He was a singer in a gospel quartet. My sister taught me how to read music.... The piano I kind of picked up, getting a fingering here, a chord there, looking over people's shoulders."

Battle's first audience was at the African Methodist Episcopal Church, where she often sang; her other audiences were at civic functions and banquets. Charles Varney, a local high school teacher recalled hearing Battle sing when she was just eight years old and what he told her: "I went to her later and told her God had blessed her, and she must always sing."

As an excellent student in school, Battle considered a career in music or mathematics, but Varney convinced her to pursue music after she graduated from Portsmouth High School in 1966. She won a National Achievement Scholarship and enrolled at the College-Conservatory of Music at the University of Cincinnati. Since she felt she would never become a major performer, she took classes in art, dance, piano, and languages to increase her job opportunities. Battle received a B.A. degree in music education in 1970, and her M.A. degree the next year. After graduation Battle taught music at inner-city elementary schools while continuing her voice training with private teachers. In 1972 she auditioned for Thomas Schippers, the conductor of the Cincinnati Symphony. He chose her to perform Brahms's *Ein Deutsches Requiem* at the Festival of Two Worlds in Spoleto, Italy.

Leaves teaching for music career

Deciding to concentrate on music full time, Battle resigned from her teaching position. She was introduced to James Levine, the music director and principal conductor of New York's Metropolitan Opera, who was a Cincinnati native. He had come home to be the visiting director at the orchestra's renowned May Festival. After auditioning Battle he was so impressed with her voice that he chose her to sing a short soprano role in Mahler's *Eighth Symphony* at the festival the next year. "Some singers have little instinct but do have the intellect to balance the technical and musical issues. Some have instinct and a beautiful voice but less intellect. I had never come across a more complete talent than hers," Levine said.

Levine encouraged Battle to develop her repertoire to include sacred music emphasizing Mozart. Battle's reputation

grew as she began making appearances across the country. She went to New York, where she was offered an understudy part in Scott Joplin's opera *Treemonisha*. In 1976 she made her operatic debut at the Michigan Opera Theater, and debuted as Susanna in *The Marriage of Figaro* with the New York City Opera. She then auditioned at the Metropolitan Opera, and two years later on September 18, 1978, she made her debut under Levine's direction as the shepherd in Wagner's *Tannhauser.*

Seven years later Battle was a top singer in opera as *Time* declared her as the "best lyric coloratura soprano in the world." She has the lyric fare of typical coloratura opera characters–Adinas, Despinas, Norinas, Zerlinas, Paminas, and Rosinas–and has also added spirituals and suitable works by Schubert, Duparc, Brahms, Haydn, Mahler, and Bach. In 1986 her recital at Alice Tully Hall in New York was sold out months in advance. Battle averages 60 performances a year, with her most memorable roles being the young servants (soubrettes) and heroines of Mozart.

Knows limits of her voice

Some music critics have charged that Battle is limited in her roles; however, the majority of them feel her confined set of roles may actually concentrate her talents. Her roles are usually confined to the soubrette and coloratura repertoires that accommodate her vocal range. "I won't stretch or pull my voice beyond its capacity and capability.... I know what the limit is," Battle has said. In a review of her album *Salzburg Recital* a critic wrote, "Artists like Battle should be cherished, and not dismissed with a vulgar sneer."

Called a difficult personality

Despite her successes, some critics have claimed Battle is difficult person, with criticism first surfacing during rehearsals with opera diva Kiri Te Kawana. They were appearing together in Strauss's *Arabella* in 1983 when Battle objected to cuts of her role as Zdenka. After consulting with members of the production staff, Battle requested that her role be restored to its entirety. Te Kawana refused her request, and the relationship between the two quickly deteriorated. Matthew A. Epstein, the producer of Handel's *Semele* at Carnegie Hall in which Battle starred, defended Battle's image. "She is not a pushover; she's a professional, liberated woman," he said. Over the years Battle became involved in other disputes with singers and administrators, leading to the termination of her contract with the Metropolitan Opera Company in 1994. During her career she has received numerous awards and Grammy nominations and an honorary doctorate from the University of Cincinnati in 1983. Eventually she would like to teach at the conservatory level, or commission music composed for soprano and small orchestra.

Where to learn more

Newsweek, February 21, 1994, p. 60.

New York Times Magazine, November 17, 1985.

Opera News, March 13, 1982; February 14, 1987.

People, March 7, 1983.

Time, November 11, 1985; February 21, 1994, p. 60.

Washington Post, March 29, 1995, p. B6.

Simone de Beauvoir

Born January 9, 1908
Paris, France
Died August 14, 1986
Paris, France
French writer
One of the prominent intellectuals
of the twentieth century

"One never sees oneself as an idol. I am Simone de Beauvoir for others, not for myself."

Simone de Beauvoir was in the French vanguard of new ideas. As the result of her lifelong love affair with the philosopher and writer Jean-Paul Sartre, Beauvoir was at the center of an influential intellectual movement and the fight against oppression. She participated in the French Resistance movement against Nazi occupation during World War II (1939-1945) and wrote about her experience in her novel *The Mandarins.* Beauvoir was also a major figure in the feminist movement, and her study of the status of women, *The Second Sex,* is regarded as a classic statement of liberation.

Grows up in middle-class family

Born on January 9, 1908, in Paris, France, the daughter of Georges Bertrand and Francoise (Brasseur) de Beauvoir, Beauvoir grew up in the fourteenth "arrondissement," or district, where she continued to live most of her life. The contrast between the devoutly Catholic, provincial, Francoise de Beau-

voir and the agnostic, cosmopolitan Parisian Georges de Beauvoir led the young Beauvoir to assess situations with an independent mind. As the family finances dwindled during World
War I (1914-1918) Beauvoir noticed the unpleasant household
chores her mother had to do. Determined never to become a
housewife or a mother, she decided to pursue a teaching career.

Loses religious faith

Despite Beauvoir's warm memories of going as a little
girl to early morning mass with her mother, she gradually
pulled away from strict religious values. With her sister she
began to rebel against the restrictions of the Cours Adeline
Desir, the private Catholic school they attended. Beauvoir's
loss of faith erected a barrier between her and her mother. At
this time the 15-year-old Beauvoir also became convinced that
she was in love with her cousin, Jacques Champigneulles,
who introduced her to some of France's best writers. Scandal-
ized by these books, her mother pinned together the pages she
did not want her daughters to read in the volumes in their
home library. Beauvoir's apparent love for Champigneulles
soured when he put aside his bohemian attitude to marry a
wealthy young woman with a generous dowry.

Meets Sartre

When Beauvoir met Sartre at a study group at the Sorbonne, the great university in Paris, her life was permanently
changed. In Sartre she found the partner about whom she had
dreamed as an adolescent. She described their meeting in one
of her memoirs: "Sartre corresponded exactly to the ideal I
had set for myself when I was fifteen: he was a soul mate in
whom I found, heated to the point of incandescence, all of my
passions. With him, I could always share everything." She and
Sartre were together for 51 years, from the time they became
acquainted in 1929 until his death on April 15, 1980.

As they grew closer Beauvoir and Sartre analyzed their
relationship, deciding that they must leave themselves open to
"contingent loves" in order to expand their range of experience.

Beauvoir and Jean-Paul Sarte in 1967 vacationing in Rome.

Although marriage would have enabled them to secure a double teaching assignment, they were not interested in compromise. Since they had no desire to have children, there was no reason to marry. This relationship troubled Beauvoir's family because it was a daring and unconventional arrangement for the early 1930s. Except for a brief period during World War II, Beauvoir and Sartre never lived together. They spent their days writing in their separate quarters and then came together during the evenings to read and criticize one another's manuscripts. When they became well-known figures in the literary world they found it difficult to maintain their privacy. For instance, the couple had to alter their routine and avoid certain cafes during the years after the war in order to protect themselves from the public.

Writes novels

Beauvoir began her writing career with a series of novels. Her first book, *She Came to Stay* (1943), is a fictional account of the experiences of Sartre's young student, Olga Kosakiewicz, who lived with Beauvoir and Sartre in an unconventional arrangement. Leaving personal concerns, Beauvoir examined philosophical issues in her next novel, *The Blood of Others* (1946). The heroine, Helene Bertrand, joins the French Resistance against the German occupation of France after she sees a little Jewish girl taken away by the Gestapo and comes to believe that violence may be the only response to Hitler. The senseless killing that took place during World War II turned Beauvoir's attention to death in *All Men Are Mortal* (1946). The novel's hero, who is immortal, wanders through seven centuries–from the thirteenth century to the twentieth century. The reader is led to conclude that immortality is no answer and that meaning in life comes from one's mortality.

Defines existentialism

Beauvoir and Sartre popularized a philosophy that came to be known as existentialism. At first Beauvoir resisted this label, but she and Sartre gradually adopted it and began to try to explain their ideas to the public. She defined existentialism as a philosophy of ambiguity, one that emphasizes the tension between living in the present and acting with an eye to one's mortality. In *Existentialism and the Wisdom of the Ages* Beauvoir wrote that a philosophical approach is needed in modern life and that, according to existentialism, which she considered an optimistic view of the human condition, people are neither naturally good nor naturally bad: "[The individual] is nothing at first; it is up to him to make himself good or bad depending upon whether he assumes his freedom or denies it."

The Second Sex

In *The Second Sex,* the work for which Beauvoir gained her reputation as an important thinker, she tries to determine how being born female had influenced the pattern of her life. Retreating to the Bibliotheque Nationale (National Library) in Paris, she conducted research for the book that was to become the battle cry of feminism. When *The Second Sex* appeared in 1949, conservative readers were horrified and women were gratified to find an honest discussion of their condition. The opening statement of the section on childhood–"One is not born a woman, one becomes one"–has become familiar throughout the world as a description of the condition of women. The book advises women to pursue meaningful careers and to avoid the status of "relative beings" that, in Beauvoir's opinion, is thrust upon them by marriage and motherhood.

Wins Goncourt Prize

After publication of *The Second Sex* Beauvoir returned to writing fiction. *The Mandarins* (1954), for which she won the prestigious Goncourt Prize, examines the disillusionment of French intellectuals. Those who had worked together during the French Resistance now saw divisions forming in what was once a united cause. Beauvoir denied the novel was a fictionalized account of Sartre, Albert Camus (an important French novelist and existential thinker), and herself, although the events in the book parallel the experiences of Beauvoir and her friends. Beauvoir next turned to her memoirs, publishing three volumes–*Memoirs of a Dutiful Daughter* (1958), *The Prime of Life* (dedicated to Sartre, 1962), and *The Force of Circumstance* (1963). In *All Said and Done* (1972) Beauvoir speculates about what her life would have been like had she not met Sartre or made certain choices. *A Very Easy Death* (1964), which is about her mother's death, and *Adieux: A Farewell to Sartre* are companion pieces that contemplate the meaning of death. By the time of her own death on August 14, 1986, in Paris, Beauvoir had become an international symbol for women in the struggle for equality and identity.

Where to learn more

Bair, Deirdre, "Do As She Said, Not As She Did," *New York Times Magazine,* November 18, 1990.

Evans, Mary, *Simone de Beauvoir: A Feminist Mandarin,* Tavistock, 1985.

Friedan, Betty, *It Changed My Life,* Random House, 1976.

Okely, Judith, *Simone de Beauvoir,* Pantheon, 1986.

Schwarzer, Alice, *After "The Second Sex": Conversations with Simone de Beauvoir,* Pantheon, 1984.

Sorel, Nancy Caldwell, "First Encounters," *The Atlantic,* November 1990, p. 119.

Jocelyn Bell Burnell

Born July 15, 1943
Belfast, Northern Ireland

Irish astronomer

Discovered pulsars and
Nobel Prize winner

Jocelyn Bell Burnell is the astronomer who discovered pulsars, for she which won the Nobel Prize in 1974. She now works on gamma-ray astronomy and infrared astronomy, as well as millimeter wave astronomy at the University of Edinburgh in Scotland.

Bell Burnell was born in Belfast, Northern Ireland, on July 15, 1943. Her father was an architect who designed the Armagh Observatory, an astronomical observatory close to their home, where her early interest in astronomy was encouraged by the observatory staff. Bell Burnell attended Mount School in York, England, and then University of Glasgow in Scotland. She earned her B.S. degree in 1965. That same year she began work on her Ph.D. under Antony Hewish at Cambridge University in England.

Starts work on quasars

Bell Burnell chose to do her doctoral work on recently discovered quasars. Specializing in radio astronomy, she spent her first two years as a graduate student building a special radio telescope designed by Hewish. Once the telescope was operating in July 1967, it was Bell Burnell's job to make sense out of the signals recorded by the instrument.

Encounters unusual problem

One day Bell Burnell noticed some curious variations in signals that had been recorded around midnight the night before. They came from the direction opposite from the sun. This seemed odd to Bell Burnell, because strong changes in signals from quasars are usually weak at night as a result of solar wind, the electrically charged material thrown out by the sun. The source of these signals gave off short bursts of energy lasting less than 1/100th of a second and occurring rapidly at precise intervals. When Bell Burnell approached Hewish, he suggested that there was a problem with the equipment or electrical interference. No one realized at the time that stars could emit radio waves that began and ended so quickly. Hewish had Bell Burnell check the instruments several more times to eliminate any possible source of interference.

Discovers pulsars

Bell Burnell found no interference and no problems with the telescope, and the scintillating (twinkling) star continued to wink at her. After a month of precise observation, she was able to establish that the signals continued and remained fixed with respect to the stars–which meant they were coming from somewhere other than the Earth or the sun. By November 1967 Bell Burnell had measured some strong, regular signals. The research team felt obliged, at least at first, to consider the possibility that the source of the signals was a beacon from some extraterrestrial civilization. They jokingly named the source of the signals "LGM 1," for Little Green Men 1. Hewish wanted to be sure that LGM 1 was not an abnormality, so he had Bell Burnell search through miles and miles of charts recorded in previous months.

Bell Burnell found three other sources with similar signals, as did her fellow team members. Hewish named the sources "pulsating stars," but the term was soon contracted to "pulsars" because they pulsated at regular intervals. After Hewish announced the discovery on February 9, 1968, some British tabloid newspapers claimed the scientists had made contact with alien civilizations. The pulsars were named for the observatories where they were found: CP for the Cambridge Pulsar, HP for the Harvard Pulsar, and so on, followed by four numbers that indicated their location in the sky.

The Hewish radio telescope

Radio telescopes have an advantage over visible-light telescopes, or optical telescopes: radio telescopes can pick up long wavelength radio waves–a form of radiation–from objects in deep space that optical telescopes cannot see. In 1964 astronomers had discovered that the radio signals given off by sources in space were not always steady, just as light from stars (visible wavelengths of radiation) appears to twinkle. This twinkling of radio signals is called scintillation and can be used to calculate the size of the radio source. The radio telescope Hewish designed was able to record time variations in the strength of radio sources.

White dwarf stars?
Neutron stars?

The biggest problem with the signals from the pulsars was the short duration of the burst and their rapid repetition. Hewish initially speculated that pulsars were either white dwarf stars or perhaps even neutron stars–stars that had been predicted but never seen. Astrophysicist Thomas Gold of Cornell University in Ithaca, New York, interpreted Bell Burnell's data and suggested that pulsars must be neutron stars resulting from the explosion of supernova. He argued that the LGM signals were from neutron stars, or small, dense spheres spinning rapidly, which would cause an intense magnetic field. Gold's theory was almost completely ignored at first, but in 1968 two other astronomers, David Staelin and Edward Reifenstein at the National Radio Astronomy Observatory at

Supernova

When a star is dying its outer parts explode, causing a bright light known to astronomers as a supernova. The inner core compresses: rather than exploding, it implodes. The star's inner mass squeezes so tightly together that it actually overcomes the forces that hold atoms together. It pulls the electrons into the nuclei, and the electrons and protons of the matter join, forming neutrons. This mass close to the center of the imploded star causes it to spin rapidly. Neutron stars would be very small in diameter, but incredibly dense with matter, 1,015 times the density of water. (The one Bell Burnell found could be only about 10 miles in diameter.)

Green Bank, West Virginia, found a pulsar they named NP 0532. It was located at the center of the Crab Nebula, the remains of an exploded supernova. The scientific community acknowledged that pulsars were indeed neutron stars.

Honored for her work

After the discovery of pulsars and the completion of her doctorate, Bell Burnell accepted a position at the University of Southampton and began working on gamma-ray astronomy, the detection of shorter wavelengths–called gamma rays–from space. From 1974 to 1982 she worked at the Mullard Space Science Laboratory in X-ray astronomy. In 1982 she was appointed senior research fellow at the Royal Observatory in Edinburgh, Scotland, where she has continued her research in detecting and analyzing radio spectra. Bell Burnell was awarded the Michelson Medal from the Franklin Institute in Philadelphia in 1973. She won the Nobel Prize in 1974, though Bell Burnell's name was not included in the citation; the J. Robert Oppenheimer Memorial Prize in 1978; the Beatrice M. Tinsley Prize from the American Astronomical Society in 1987; and the Herschel Medal from the Royal Astronomical Society in 1989. Bell Burnell is a member of the Royal Astronomical Society and the International Astronomical Union. In 1968 she married and now has one child.

Where to learn more

Fisher, David E., *The Origin and Evolution of Our Own Particular Universe,* Atheneum, 1988, pp. 94-99.

Halperin, Paul, *Cosmic Wormholes: The Search for Interstellar Shortcuts,* Dutton, 1992, pp. 45-48.

Mary McLeod Bethune

Born July 10, 1875
Mayesville, South Carolina

Died May 18, 1955
Daytona Beach, Florida

African American educator,
government official, and activist

Established Bethune-Cookman College,
founded National Council of Negro
Women, held positions in President
Franklin D. Roosevelt's administration

Mary McLeod Bethune rose from poverty to become one of the nation's most distinguished African American leaders and the most prominent black woman of her time. Her life encompassed three different careers: she was the central figure in the creation of Bethune-Cookman College in Daytona Beach, Florida; she was the founder and president of the National Council of Negro Women; and she was one of the few blacks to hold influential positions in President Franklin D. Roosevelt's administration.

Born in 1875 near Mayesville, South Carolina, Bethune was the 15th of 17 children. Her parents were former slaves freed at the time of the Civil War (1861-1865) who instilled their strong religious values and work ethic in Bethune when she was young. Bethune's education began at a free school near Mayesville. Then she received a scholarship to Scotia Seminary (later Barber-Scotia College), in Concord, North Carolina, where the racially mixed faculty was Bethune's first intellectual exposure to whites. After graduating from Scotia, Bethune

"Be calm,
be steadfast,
be courageous."

enrolled at the Bible Institute for Home and Foreign Missions (now the Moody Bible Institute) in Chicago, again with a scholarship. Finishing her studies in 1895, she took a teaching job at the Haines Normal and Industrial Institute in Augusta, Georgia.

Starts a school

After a year at Haines, Bethune returned to her native South Carolina to teach at the Kindell Institute in Sumter. There she met Albertus Bethune, a former teacher who had become a menswear salesman. After marrying in 1898 they moved to Savannah, Georgia. Bethune retired temporarily from teaching to give birth to their only child, Albert McLeod Bethune, in 1899. Later that year the family moved to Palatka, Florida, where Bethune opened the Palatka Mission School. Her husband did not share her missionary zeal, however, and the couple separated.

In 1904 Bethune moved to Daytona Beach, where construction of the Florida East Coast Railway was attracting and employing large numbers of black laborers. She later recalled her arrival in Daytona Beach, saying she found "ignorance and meager educational facilities, social prejudice, and crime. This was the place to plant my seed." Reportedly beginning with only $1.50 in savings, Bethune rented a four-room cottage and opened her school with six pupils–five girls and her son. She raised additional money by soliciting funds door to door. Most school furnishings came from the city dump, and students collected and repaired used and discarded items like chairs, desks, rugs, and dishes.

Realizes her dream

Bethune's powerful personality and shrewd business skills soon made the Daytona Normal and Industrial Institute a phenomenal success. At first, like most black schools of the time, the institute stressed religion and industrial training, that is, the learning of trade skills for future employment. But as time went on the Daytona Institute began to devote more attention to its high school programs and to encouraging ambitious students to attend college. In 1911, after her students were refused service in Daytona Beach's whites-only hospital, Bethune established a hospital alongside the school. She also defied the local Ku Klux Klan, a secret society that advocates white supremacy, by leading a successful black voter registration drive in 1920.

Becomes a college president

By 1923 the Daytona Institute had an enrollment of 300. Bethune expanded the school into a college for the training of future teachers, merging it with the Cookman Institute, a Jacksonville men's college. She became the first president of the new institution, which was officially renamed Bethune-Cookman College in 1929. Bethune traveled throughout the United States soliciting funds for the school, often using her talent as a singer and orator to charm potential donors. She also began her rise to national prominence through her work in organizing the black women's club movement. In 1924 she became president of the 10,000-member National Association of Colored Women, at that time thought to be the highest position a black woman could achieve.

Promotes dignity of black women

During her travels Bethune worked to project a positive image of black women. She made countless speeches and defended the dignity of black women by refusing to answer to "Auntie," or other derogatory names common during the era. In 1935 she created the National Council of Negro Women, a coalition of organizations and concerned individuals that assists in the development of the leadership of women in community, national, and international life. In addition, she worked with the Southern Conference for Human Welfare, the National Urban League, and the National Association for the Advancement of Colored People, which presented her with its Spingarn Medal for distinguished achievement. Through her club work Bethune met first lady **Eleanor Roosevelt** (see entry), and in 1935 the president's wife used her influence to

have Bethune appointed to the National Advisory Committee of the National Youth Administration (NYA). Established as part of the New Deal, President Roosevelt's ambitious program to bring the country out of the Great Depression, the NYA helped young people find employment.

In 1936 Bethune brought together blacks who held positions in the Roosevelt administration to discuss how to secure a better life for African Americans under the New Deal. The group became known as the "black cabinet." Bethune promoted civil rights reforms by marching and picketing Washington, D.C., businesses that refused to hire blacks. She also supported drives to free the Scottsboro Boys–nine young black men who were unjustly accused and tried for raping two white women on a freight train and were tried in Scottsboro, Alabama, in 1931.

Remains active in final years

Ill health forced Bethune to give up the presidency of Bethune-Cookman College in 1942. When the NYA disbanded in 1943, she left government service, but served as special representative of the U.S. State Department at the 1945 San Francisco Conference that established the United Nations. Until her death from a heart attack in 1955 Bethune remained the most influential black woman in the United States, receiving national and international awards for her work. In commemoration of her leadership a statue was later dedicated in Lincoln Park, in Washington, D.C. It was the first such honor for a woman or a black in a public park in the nation's capital.

Where to learn more

Greene, Carol, *Mary McLeod Bethune: Champion for Education,* Childrens Press, 1993.

Halasa, Malu, *Mary McLeod Bethune,* Chelsea House, 1989.

McKissack, Pat, *Mary McLeod Bethune,* Childrens Press, 1992.

McKissack, Pat, *Mary McLeod Bethune: A Great Teacher,* Enslow Publishers, 1991.

Benazir Bhutto

Born June 21, 1953
Karachi, Pakistan
Pakistani chief executive
First woman prime minister
of a Muslim country

"As a daughter of the East I want other women, born into this tradition ... to see how I fight– as a politician, as a woman, as a mother– and how I survive."

Upon her election as prime minister of Pakistan in 1988, Benazir Bhutto became the first woman in modern history to be the chief executive of a predominantly Muslim country and one of the youngest prime ministers in the world. Until that moment, however, she had undergone five harrowing years of imprisonment and house arrest, followed by two years of exile as well as numerous conspiracies and attempts on her life. By winning the prime ministry she had vindicated the death of her father, the first popularly elected prime minister in the history of Pakistan (1973-1977), who was executed by political enemies in 1979. Although Bhutto remained in office only 20 months, she was reelected in 1993.

Long political heritage

Bhutto was born on June 21, 1953, in Karachi, Pakistan, the eldest of four children of Zulfikar Ali Bhutto and his second wife, Nusrat Isphahani, who was an Iranian. The Bhuttos were a prominent political family who had accepted the Islam religion. Bhutto's grandfather was a leader in the Indian colonial government before Pakistan became an independent nation. Her father, who was known as Zulfi, held various offices in the Pakistani government prior to founding the Pakistan Political Party (PPP) in 1967 and being named president in 1971. Throughout her childhood and teenage years Bhutto led a privileged, protected life. Her father trained her to be his political heir, introducing her to important world leaders and tutoring her in the art of politics. When she was 16 Zulfi sent her to be educated at Radcliffe College, which is affiliated with Harvard University in Cambridge, Massachusetts. At first she was homesick and hated the cold weather, but eventually she enjoyed socializing with ordinary girls her own age.

While Bhutto was at Radcliffe she continued to be part of her father's inner circle, at one point meeting **Indira Gandhi** (see entry), who became her own father's successor. Bhutto graduated with a bachelor of arts degree in 1973, the same year Zulfi Bhutto became the first popularly elected prime minister in the history of Pakistan. Bhutto went on to the University of Oxford in England to study political science, economics, and international affairs, receiving another bachelor of arts degree in 1977. While at Oxford she was head of the Oxford Union, a debating society, and she had tea with **Margaret Thatcher** (see entry), who was embarking on a political career. Bhutto was a glamorous figure at Oxford as she sped around town in a yellow sports car.

Terror and imprisonment

When Bhutto returned to Pakistan from England in 1977, she had planned to enter the foreign service. However, she found the country in political chaos as street protests raged against Zulfi Bhutto's newly elected government, which was soon overthrown by the army chief of staff, Mohammad Zia ul-Haq. Her life changed dramatically. Shortly after Zia seized power the entire Bhutto family was imprisoned. In March 1978 Zulfi Bhutto was sentenced to death for ordering the assassination of a political opponent three years earlier. Bhutto committed herself to his defense, urging his claims of innocence, but he was executed in April 1979. The only people permitted to visit him in his final hours were his wife and Benazir, his firstborn and favorite child.

After the execution, Bhutto's brothers, Mir Murtaza and Shah Nawaz, escaped to Afghanistan, while her sister Sanam went into exile in London, England, and her mother went into exile in France. Bhutto herself remained in Pakistan and became the head of the PPP. For a period of five years, until 1984, Zia put her under house arrest or had her moved to jails throughout the country. In 1981 she was placed in total isolation for five months in a cage-like cell, where her health deteriorated. In interviews and in her autobiography, *Daughter of Destiny,* which was published in 1989, Bhutto has described the humiliation of confinement: "Even now, though so many years have passed, I shudder to think of it. It was like being buried alive in a grave. You live, yet you don't live.... I discovered later that I'd become anorexic, and, as though that weren't enough, my teeth began to rot and my hair fell out."

Exile and return

Bhutto went into exile in Britain in 1984. The following year she again experienced tragedy when she found her younger and favorite brother, Shah Nawaz, the victim of apparent poisoning, dead on the floor of his apartment in Cannes, France. In 1986 she returned to the Islamabad, the capital of Pakistan, after the lifting of martial law and moved to the forefront of opposition against Zia. Then a year later, at the age of 34, she agreed to an arranged marriage with Asif Ali Zardari, who was chosen by her aunt. Many of her friends thought her decision unusual–after all, she was an independent woman who could marry for love–but she said it was politically wise to wed someone she did not know. Although Zardari became a member of the national assembly, he devotes most of his time to business concerns. Bhutto and Zardari now have three children.

Rise to power

In August 1988, when Zia died in a mysterious plane crash, Bhutto took advantage of the vacuum his death had caused in Pakistani politics. In the subsequent elections her PPP won the largest number of seats in the national assembly. The following December Bhutto was elected prime minister, heading a coalition government and becoming only the second prime minister, after her father, to win the office by popular vote. Once she was in power her first step was to free political prisoners and restore civil rights. A popular leader, she modeled herself after **Eva Perón** (see entry) and **Corazon Aquino** (see entry), both of whom cultivated the support of the working classes. She also maintained her friendship with Thatcher, who was now Great Britain's first woman prime minister. However, Bhutto was not able to overcome Pakistan's widespread problems, such as poverty, government corruption, and rampant crime. In August 1990 the president of Pakistan, Ishaq Khan, dismissed Bhutto's government on

Bhutto and President Bill Clinton at a press conference in 1995.

charges of corruption and other wrongdoing, calling for new elections. Bhutto lost the election, which she contends was rigged, to Nawaz Sharif, a millionaire and protégé of Khan.

Second term as prime minister

As soon as Bhutto left office she began campaigning to win it back. Staging a series of "long marches" in the streets of Islamabad, she gathered hundreds of thousands of supporters who demanded new elections. When Khan dismissed Sharif on charges of corruption, an opening was left for Bhutto. In April 1993 new elections were held and she won her second term as prime minister. Taking advantage of her connections in the West, she has since worked to improve Pakistan's relations with Europe and the United States. In 1995 Bhutto met with President Bill Clinton and addressed the United States Congress, becoming the first Pakistani prime minister to visit the United States since the end of the cold war (a period of power struggles between western and communist countries that began after World War II [1939-1945] and lasted until 1989).

Where to learn more

Bhutto, Benazir, *Daughter of Destiny: An Autobiography,* Simon & Schuster, 1989.

Bouchard, Elizabeth, *Benazir Bhutto: Prime Minister,* Blackbirch Press, 1992.

New York Times, April 12, 1995, p. A1, p. A5.

Weaver, Mary Anne, "Bhutto's Fateful Moment," *New Yorker,* October 4, 1993.

Shirley Temple Black

Born April 23, 1928
Santa Monica, California
American actress and diplomat
Popular child star and
U.S. ambassador to Ghana

During her childhood in the 1930s Academy Award-winner Shirley Temple Black was the most popular star in American films. Bubbly and curly-haired, with the face of a dimple-cheeked cherub, she was known as "America's sweetheart." The grim conditions of the Great Depression, a period of severe economic crisis, made audiences eager to see her in films with happy endings that helped them forget their own troubles. As an adult she became the U.S. ambassador to Ghana and the first woman chief of protocol in U.S. history.

Baby movie star

Black was born Shirley Jane Temple on April 23, 1928, in Santa Monica, California, the third of three children of George Francis, a banker, and Gertrude Creiger Temple. She began her acting career at the age of three and a half. Gertrude Temple provided her two-year-old daughter with dancing and singing lessons, then signed a contract for her with Education-

"I class myself with Rin Tin Tin [a popular canine film star]; people in the Depression wanted something to cheer them up, and they fell in love with a dog and a little girl."

al Films Corporation for $40 a week in 1932. Temple soon appeared in two series of short films titled "Baby Burlesks" and "Frolics of Youth." Her first words in a film were "*Oui, mon cher*" (French for "Yes, my dear"). When her agent appeared to lose interest in the aspiring young star, her mother was able to get a contract with Fox Film Corporation (now Twentieth-Century Fox) at $150 a week. In 1932, at the age of four, Temple made her debut in a full-length film, *The Red-haired Alibi.* Within two years she had gained critical attention in *Stand Up and Cheer.* Her first starring role came that same year in a production of *Little Miss Marker,* which began a stream of movies, including *The Little Colonel, Poor Little Rich Girl, Rebecca of Sunnybrook Farm,* and *The Little Princess,* among others.

"Outstanding personality of 1934"

At the peak of Temple's popularity in 1934 the Ideal Toy and Novelty Company in New York marketed a Shirley Temple doll for the Christmas season. Thousands were sold. Her successful films lifted Fox Film Corporation out of a financial crisis brought on by the depression, and in 1935 she became the first child actor to win an Academy Award. Presenting her an Oscar scaled down to child size especially for her, the American Academy of Motion Picture Arts and Sciences named her "the outstanding personality of 1934." The studio attempted to capitalize on Temple's popular image as long as possible by dressing her in clothes often too young for her age. Her standard costume was a ruffled, frilly dress with so many petticoats underneath that the skirt stuck straight out, and since she danced in most of her films she also wore tap shoes and ankle socks. Yet at the same time she was cast as "miniature adults." For instance, in one of the "Baby Burlesk" movies for Educational Films she played a French girl and wore a blouse with one bare shoulder and a rose in her hair. In another she played the film goddess Marlene Dietrich, wearing a slinky sequined gown.

The Little Colonel (1935) caused a stir when Temple appeared in a dance scene with the famous black dancer Bill

"Bojangles" Robinson. As she recalls in her autobiography,
Child Star, "Gooseflesh did rise among some preview audiences, notably in southern states. In our staircase dance we
touched fingers. To avoid social offense and assure wide dis-
tribution, the studio cut scenes showing physical contact
between us. But for the rest of the world we provided a watershed. We were the first interracial couple in movie history."

Shirley Temple Black

Although her films are generally regarded as sugary, sentimental attempts to help adult audiences temporarily escape the depression, critics have praised her acting and dancing performances, noting that she had a rare natural talent.

A fortune gained and lost

As Temple grew older she became less popular and in 1940 Fox terminated her contract. She made several other films for Metro-Goldwyn-Mayer (MGM), then she appeared in three "Shirley Temple" television series in the mid-1940s. By that time, however, she was interested in other pursuits. In 1945 she married John Agar, Jr., with whom she had a daughter, Susan. After she and Agar divorced in 1949 she married Charles A. Black, with whom she has had a happy union and two children, Lois and Charles, Jr. Not long after her wedding Black discovered that her father had lost almost all of the $3 million she had earned from her films. She later commented that she was not bitter toward him: "I don't blame my dad," she said. "He dropped out of school at 14. He was extremely generous with loaning money." Instead she began to focus her energies on politics. In 1967 she ran for the U.S. Congress as a representative from California, adopting a conservative platform and insisting that she was running on the issues rather than her name. Although she lost the election she placed second in a field of 10 candidates.

Diplomatic career

Black continued to be active in politics, and in 1969 President Richard Nixon appointed her as the U.S. representative to the 24th General Assembly of the United Nations (UN). Although she had cancer surgery three years later, she continued her involvement in the UN, serving as assistant to the chairman of the Council on Environmental Equality. In 1974 President Gerald Ford appointed her as the U.S. ambassador to Ghana in Africa, a post she held for two years. She recalled this as one of the happiest times of her life: "I had to use all the communication skills, people skills, and problem-

Selected films starring Shirley Temple

Little Miss Marker (**1934**) A heartwarming story about a little girl who is the IOU (I owe you) for a gambling debt.

The Little Colonel (**1935**) After the Civil War an embittered Southern gentleman turns his back on his family, until his dimple-cheeked granddaughter softens his heart.

Poor Little Rich Girl (**1936**) A motherless rich girl wanders away from home and is "adopted" by two struggling vaudevillians. With her help they rise to the big time.

Heidi (**1937**) Johanna Spyri's classic tale puts Temple in the hands of a mean governess and the loving arms of her Swiss grandfather.

Rebecca of Sunnybrook Farm (**1938**) Temple becomes a radio star over her aunt's objections in this bouncy musical (not based on the book by Daphne du Maurier).

The Little Princess (**1939**) Considered Temple's best film, *The Little Princess* is based on the classic children's novel by **Frances Hodgson Burnett** (see entry) about a young schoolgirl in Victorian London who is sent to a harsh boarding school.

solving skills that I had ever learned." Her experiences as a film star, which had given her the opportunity to meet such important figures as President Franklin Roosevelt and **Eleanor Roosevelt** (see entry), were also useful in her new diplomatic career. Yet her success in Ghana can also be attributed to her sociable personality. While in Africa, for instance, she once participated in a folk dance in a village marketplace, and she frequently wore African-print dresses. In 1977, recognizing Black's talent for foreign relations, President Gerald Ford appointed her chief of protocol. She was the first woman in U.S. history to hold that post.

Continued service

While Black was the U.S. ambassador to Czechoslovakia in 1989 she witnessed the "velvet revolution" that resulted in the fall of the 21-year-old Communist regime and which made the playwright Vaclav Havel head of the new democratic government. This event held special significance for Black because she had been in Prague, Czechoslovakia, in 1968 when Soviet tanks moved into the city to take over the country. Black later became a founding member and officer of the Board of Directors of the American Academy of Diplomacy in Washington, D.C. She has served as a member of the U.S. Commission for UNESCO (United Nations Educational, Scientific, and Cultural Organization) and as a foreign affairs officer for the Foreign Affairs Institute of the U.S. Department of State. She is the director of the National Multiple Sclerosis Society, which combats the disease that afflicted her brother George. Black has received many honors, including the Cross of Malta and the American Exemplar Medal.

Where to learn more

Black, Shirley Temple, *Child Star: An Autobiography,* McGraw-Hill, 1988.

Cadden, Vivian, "Return to Prague," *McCall's,* April 1990, pp. 60-63+.

Edwards, Anne, *Shirley Temple: American Princess,* Morrow, 1988.

Haskins, James, *Shirley Temple Black: Actress to Ambassador,* Viking Kestrel, 1988.

Elizabeth H. Blackburn

Born November 26, 1948
Hobart, Australia

Australian-born American
molecular biologist

Discovered telomerase, an enzyme necessary
for cell division; named foreign associate
of the National Academy of Sciences

Elizabeth H. Blackburn is a molecular biologist and biochemist who conducted ground-breaking research on deoxyribonucleic acid (DNA) and cell division that has provided a new line of inquiry into the chemical bases of life. Her discovery of a key enzyme, telomerase, which is necessary for chromosomes to make copies of themselves before cell division, has been applied to the study of chromosome behavior as well as certain diseases such as fungal infections and cancer. Widely recognized as one of the top researchers in her field, Blackburn is the first woman to head the Department of Microbiology and Immunology at the University of California at San Francisco.

Early life

Blackburn was born in Hobart, Australia, on November 26, 1948. Her early interest in medicine and biology was influenced by her parents, Harold Blackburn and Marcia

DNA

Chromosomes are thread-like structures in the nucleus of a cell that carry thousands of genes. Both chromosomes and genes are made of deoxyribonucleic acid, or DNA, the hereditary material found in all organisms, except for some viruses. DNA is a long molecule composed of two chains of nucleotides, or organic chemicals, that contain the sugar deoxyribose.

(Jack) Blackburn, both of whom were physicians. Blackburn graduated from the University of Melbourne with a B.S. degree in 1970 and an M.S. degree in 1971. She received a Ph.D. in molecular biology from Cambridge University in Cambridge, England, in 1975. Blackburn then moved to the United States, where some of the most exciting opportunities and advances in molecular biology were being made. In 1975 she also married John Sedat, an American she had met at Cambridge; he had earned his doctoral degree and was pursuing research in biology. They have one son, Benjamin.

Starts pioneering research

Blackburn was awarded a fellowship in biology at Yale University in New Haven, Connecticut, to work with Joseph Gall in chromosome research. Blackburn began her work with telomeres, which help chromosomes to remain stable and whole during the DNA replication (duplication) cycle. In 1978 Blackburn became assistant professor at the University of California at Berkeley, where she was to make her groundbreaking discoveries concerning chromosomes and DNA.

Discovers telomerase

Blackburn was studying the DNA sequences in telomeres and chromosome structures in eukaryotes (one of two types of cells with a well-defined nucleus containing rodlike chromosomes) when she observed that the chromosomes appeared to shrink and grow in length. Intrigued, Blackburn set out to solve this biological riddle. She found that, in order to survive, cells had developed a process to replace lost telomeres. Specifically, she discovered an unusual key enzyme, telomerase, which is necessary for chromosomes to make complete copies of themselves before cell division.

In first studying the single-celled protozoan *Tetrahymena,* Blackburn removed its telomerase and found that the DNA progressively shortened until it died. She discovered that telomerase makes DNA from a ribonucleic acid (RNA) template, or pattern. Blackburn has used her discoveries to make artificial chromosomes for studying chromosome behavior and telomere synthesis. Such studies on the RNA of telomerase could help determine how the earliest forms of life evolved and could be useful in the fight against fungal diseases and cancer.

Honored for her achievements

After 12 years at Berkeley, in 1990 Blackburn became professor of microbiology and immunology at the University of California at San Francisco. In July 1993 she became the first woman chair of the university's Department of Microbiology and Immunology. Having achieved worldwide eminence in the field of molecular biology, Blackburn was named a foreign associate to the National Academy of Sciences. This is one of the highest honors that can be given a scientist in the United States. She has also won the National Academy of Sciences Award in molecular biology and is a fellow of the Royal Society, an independent organization in the United Kingdom.

Telomerase

Without telomeres, daughter cells, or copies, will have shortened versions of chromosomes from the parent cells and will eventually die. Telomerase is an unusual enzyme because it contains RNA, which is involved in the synthesis of proteins in all organisms. It is also the hereditary material of some viruses. Telomerase adds DNA onto the end of the *Tetrahymena* chromosome to preserve it, thus preventing eventual cell death and ensuring the completion of cell division.

Bonnie Blair

Born March 18, 1964
Cornwall, New York

American speed skater

First woman in U.S. history to win Gold Medals at three consecutive Olympic games; first American woman to win five Olympic Gold Medals; American with the most medals in the Winter Olympics

"Skating is joy. It's a solitary sport, one in which you can claim all the rewards as your own. Nobody makes you do it. It's just you."

Speed skater Bonnie Blair is the first woman in U.S. history to win Gold Medals at three consecutive Olympic games. In 1994 she became the first American woman to win five Gold Medals overall in the Olympics, winter or summer. A Bronze Medal added to her Gold gave her more medals in the Winter Olympics than any other American. Shorter and less powerful than some of her Olympic rivals, Blair perfected a technique that helped her set the world record for the 500-meter speed skating race.

Grows up in skating environment

Blair was born March 18, 1964, in Cornwall, New York, the youngest of six children. Her entire family loved to speed skate, and Blair was actually born while her brothers and sisters were involved in a local speed skating event. On the way to the race her father left her mother at the hospital, and Blair's birth was announced at the rink. By age two Blair was already skating, wearing skates over her street shoes. "I can't even remember learning how to skate. It comes almost as naturally to me as walking," she has said. In 1966 the Blair family moved to Champaign, Illinois, where skating is a popular sport. As soon as she was old enough, Blair entered her first competition, at the age of four. Three years later she raced in the Illinois state championships.

First Olympics

Blair was discovered by Cathy Priestner, a former Olympic Silver medalist in speed skating from Canada. Recognizing Blair's talent, Priestner convinced her to give up pack-style racing and work toward qualifying for the Olympics. When Blair was 16 she entered her first Olympic-style race at a qualifying meet for the 1980 Olympic trials. She was an immediate sensation. Skating the last meet, she was forced to race alone when her competitor did not appear. Blair knew she would have to skate the 500 meters in under 47 seconds to win. Although she qualified to participate in the Olympic trials, Blair did not make the 1980 Olympic team. Refusing to become discouraged, Blair looked ahead to the 1984 games.

Brain over brawn

Being 5 feet 5 inches tall and weighing 125 pounds, Blair was smaller than her competitors, especially the women from East Germany. She therefore decided to concentrate less on power and worked to make her technique as perfect as possible. She qualified for the 1984 Winter Olympics in Sarajevo, Yugoslavia, where she finished eighth in the 500-meter race, a good finish for a first-time Olympian. Blair's Olympic experience made her even more determined to win a medal. In 1985 she began a training program that included long skating ses-

Pack style versus free style

Blair began by competing in pack style, or short track, races: Contestants run together until they reach the last lap, when each skater then tries to break from the pack to reach the finish line first. In long track, or metric skating, only two skaters are allowed on the track at one time. The skater with the fastest time in the competition is the winner.

Blair skates for the gold during the 1992 Winter Olympics in Albertville, France.

sions, weight training, running, biking, and roller skating. In the 1985-1986 World Cup, an international competition made up of several meets, she placed fourth in the 500-meter, 1,000-meter, and 1,500-meter events.

The following year Blair broke the world record for 500 meters with a time of 39.43 seconds, winning all but one of the races she entered of that distance. She also won the World

Cup Championship. From 1985 to 1990 Blair was the U.S. champion in sprint races, which include the 500-meter, 1,000-meter, and 1,500-meter distances. Among her chief competitors was Christa Rothenburger of East Germany, the 1984 Olympic 500-meter Gold medalist. Between 1985 and 1987, Blair and Rothenburger took turns breaking the record for the 500-meter race. The stage was set for an exciting 1988 Olympic encounter between the two in Calgary, Alberta, Canada.

Olympic champion

Blair was nervous before her first race, and became more so when she watched Rothenburger earn a new world record with a time of 39.12 seconds in the 500-meter race. Blair went onto the ice to skate the race of her life and broke the world record with a time of 39.10 seconds! A few days later Blair won the Bronze Medal in the 1,000-meter sprint. Blair's teammates honored her by letting her carry the American flag at the closing ceremonies of the Olympics. After the 1988 Olympics, Blair gave up speed skating for a short time to compete in cycling, but soon returned to speed skating. She won her first World Sprint Championship in 1989 and the following year began to work with a new coach, 1976 Olympic champion Peter Mueller.

Olympian repeat

Entering the 1992 Olympics in Albertville, France, Blair was heavily favored to win the 500-meter race, even though bronchitis (a respiratory infection) had slowed her down the previous year. On a track that had begun to melt, Blair defended her Olympic title with a relatively slow time of 40.33 sec-

Police raise funds

Blair began to train with Olympic team coach Mike Crowe but was soon faced with financial difficulties. Speed skating is an expensive sport that requires travel to foreign countries and large fees for private coaches and use of skating rinks. To help with costs, the Champaign Police Department began collecting money for her expenses in 1982 and continued for almost ten years. They sold T-shirts and bumper stickers that read: Champaign Policemen's Favorite Speeder: Olympian Bonnie Blair.

onds. She dedicated the medal to her father, who had died in 1989. With her victory she became the first American woman to win Gold Medals in two straight Winter Olympics. Blair went on to face old rivals Rothenburger and Ye Qiaobo of China in the 1,000-meter competition. She won the Gold Medal, beating Ye Qiaobo by just 0.02 of a second.

Record breaker

Blair entered the 1994 Winter Olympics in Lilehammer, Norway, where she won the 500-meter race and, four days later, the 1,000-meter race. When Blair received her Gold Medal for the 1,000 meters, she cried as the U.S. national anthem was played, because she realized 1994 would be her last Olympics. Blair continued to race for another year so she could end her career at the 1995 World Sprint Championships in Milwaukee, Wisconsin, her training site.

Where to learn more

Breitenbucher, Cathy, *Bonnie Blair: Golden Streak,* Lerner Publications, 1994.

Maclean's, February 1988.

People, February 15, 1988.

Sporting News, March 7, 1994

Sports Illustrated, February 17, 1992; February 24, 1992.

Katharine Burr Blodgett

Born January 10, 1898
Schenectady, New York

Died October 12, 1979
Schenectady, New York

American chemist

Inventor of nonreflecting glass;
first woman scientist with the
General Electric Company

The inventor of invisible, or nonreflecting, glass, Katharine Burr Blodgett made several significant contributions to the field of industrial chemistry. The first woman to become a General Electric (GE) scientist, Blodgett spent nearly all of her professional life working in the GE plant in Schenectady, New York. Although Blodgett's name has little household recognition, some of the techniques in surface chemistry that she and her supervisor and mentor Irving Langmuir developed are still used in laboratories. In addition, Blodgett's invisible glass is used extensively in camera and optical equipment today.

Blodgett was born January 10, 1898, in Schenectady, New York. Her parents had moved to Schenectady earlier in the decade from their native New England. Blodgett's father, George Bedington Blodgett, became the head of the patent department at the GE plant. Blodgett never knew her father, who died a few weeks before she was born. Left widowed with two small children, Blodgett's mother, Katharine Buchanan Burr,

The fruits of Blodgett's discovery of nonreflecting glass can be found in camera lenses, automobile windows, showcases, eyeglasses, and picture frames.

decided to move to New York City. Three years later she moved the family to France so her children would become bilingual. After a few years of French schooling, Blodgett spent a year at an American school in Saranac Lake, New York, followed by travel in Germany. While in her mid-teens Blodgett returned with her family to New York City, where she attended the now-defunct Rayson School. Blodgett later won a scholarship to the all-women's Bryn Mawr College in Bryn Mawr, Pennsylvania, where she excelled in mathematics and physics.

Begins research career

After college Blodgett decided on a career in scientific research. During Christmas vacation of her senior year, she traveled to upstate New York to explore employment opportunities at the Schenectady GE plant. Some of her father's former colleagues introduced her to research chemist Irving Langmuir, winner of a 1932 Nobel Prize. After showing her the laboratory, Langmuir told 18-year-old Blodgett that she would need to broaden her scientific education before coming to work for him.

In 1918 Blodgett enrolled in the University of Chicago to pursue a master's degree in science. Since she knew that a job awaited her in industrial research, she picked a related thesis subject: the chemical structure of gas masks. Blodgett returned to GE after graduating, and Langmuir hired her as his assistant, making her the first female research scientist GE had ever employed. At the time Langmuir, who had worked on vacuum pumps and light bulbs early in his GE career, had turned his attention to studying current flow under restricted conditions. After Blodgett started working with Langmuir on these studies, they wrote several papers about their work between 1918 and 1924. Blodgett's collaboration with the Nobel laureate lasted until Langmuir died in 1957.

Invents color gauge

Blodgett realized she would need a doctorate to advance her career at GE. Six years after Blodgett started working for Langmuir, he arranged for her to pursue doctoral studies in physics at Cambridge University's Cavendish Laboratory in

England. Blodgett needed her mentor's help to gain admission to Cavendish because laboratory administrators hesitated to give one of their few open spots to a woman. With Langmuir's endorsement, however, Blodgett was able to persuade the Cambridge physicists to approve her entrance. In 1926 Blodgett became the first woman ever to receive a doctorate in physics from Cambridge University.

When Blodgett returned to Schenectady, Langmuir encouraged her to refine some of his earlier discoveries. First he set her to work on perfecting tungsten filaments, the thin wires used to conduct electricity in electric lamps (the work for which he had received a patent in 1916). Langmuir later asked Blodgett to concentrate her studies on surface chemistry. In his own long-standing research on the subject, Langmuir had discovered that oily substances formed a one-molecule-thin film when spread on water. By floating a waxed thread in front of molecules of stearic acid (a white crystal-like fatty acid derived from tallow), Langmuir had shown that this film was

Blodgett experimenting in General Electric Company's laboratory.

Katharine Burr Blodgett

A valuable scientific instrument

Not long after Blodgett's discovery, General Electric started marketing a more sophisticated version of her color gauge for use in scientific laboratories. The gauge was comprised of a sealed glass tube that contained a 6-inch strip on which layers of molecules had formed. To measure the thickness of a film only a few millionths of an inch thick, the user compares the color of the film with the molecular layers, or grades. The gauge could measure the thickness of transparent or semitransparent substances within 1- to 20-millionths of an inch as effectively as much more expensive optical instruments. It became a useful device for physicists, chemists, and metallurgists (scientists who study the technology and science of metals).

created by the active ends of the molecules resting on the surface of the water.

Blodgett decided to see what would happen if she dipped a metal plate into the molecules. Attracted to the metal, a layer of molecules formed that was similar to that which had formed on the water. As she inserted the plate into the solution again and again, Blodgett noticed that additional layers, which were all one molecule thick, formed on top of one another. As the layers formed, different colors appeared on the surface, colors that could be used to gauge the number of layers in the coating. Because this measurement was always constant, Blodgett realized she could use the plate as a gauge for measuring the thickness of a film within one microinch.

Invents invisible glass

Blodgett continued working in the field of surface chemistry. Within five years she had found another practical application that resulted from Langmuir's original studies: nonreflecting glass. Blodgett discovered that coating sheets of ordinary glass with exactly 44 layers of one-molecule-thick transparent liquid soap made the glass invisible. This overall layer of soap was four-millionths of an inch thick and one-quarter the wavelength of white light. It neutralized the light rays coming from the bottom of the glass with those coming from the top so that no light was reflected. Since the transparent soap coating blocked only about 1 percent of the light coming in, invisible glass was perfect for use in optical equipment such as cameras and telescopes.

Blodgett could not claim sole credit for creating invisible glass. Two days after she announced her discovery, two physicists at the Massachusetts Institute of Technology (MIT) publicized their method of manufacturing nonreflecting glass. Both groups of scientists, however, were concerned that their coatings were not hard and permanent enough for industrial use. Using some of Blodgett's insights, the MIT scientists eventually found a more appropriate method of producing invisible glass. Today, the fruits of Blodgett's discovery can be found in almost all lenses used in cameras and other optical equipment, as well as automobile windows, showcases, eyeglasses, picture frames, and submarine periscopes.

During World War II (1939-1945), GE moved away from studies such as the one that had led to invisible glass in favor of tackling problems for the military. Blodgett temporarily postponed her glass research but did not move far from the field of surface chemistry. Her wartime experiments led to breakthroughs in the design of the airplane wing, and she designed a smoke screen that saved lives during military campaigns.

Receives Garvan Medal

When the war ended, Blodgett continued doing military-related research. In 1947, for example, she worked with the Army Signal Corps, putting her thin-film knowledge to use by developing an instrument that could be placed in weather balloons to measure humidity in the upper atmosphere. As Blodgett worked, praise for her research continued to pour in. Along with receiving numerous honorary degrees, she won the 1945 Annual Achievement Award from the American Association of University Women for her research in surface chemistry. In 1951 she accepted the Francis P. Garvan Medal from the American Chemical Society, and she was the only scientist honored in Boston's First Assembly of American Women in Achievement. Spending all of her adult life in her home overlooking her birthplace, she remained active in civic affairs. Blodgett died at age 81 on October 12, 1979.

Where to learn more

Golemba, Beverly, *Lesser Known Women: A Biographical Dictionary,* Lynne Rienner, 1992.

O'Neill, Lois Decker, editor, *Women's Book of World Records and Achievements,* Anchor Press, 1979.

Ethel Blondin-Andrew

Born March 25, 1951
Fort Norman, Northwest Territories, Canada

Native American cabinet minister

*First Native woman elected to sit in
the Canadian House of Commons*

*"Because of
my grandmother's
influence, I always
felt that I was equal
to anybody."*

Ethel Blondin-Andrew, a Dene Indian from the Arctic region of Canada, was the first Native woman to sit in the Canadian House of Commons. Elected by a landslide victory in 1988 to represent the western Arctic, Blondin-Andrew was named secretary of state for youth and training by Prime Minister Jean Chretien in November 1993. As a high-profile cabinet minister, Blondin-Andrew campaigned for the rights of aborigines, or native people, and defended trapping and the fur industry.

Describing herself as a "snotty-nosed kid from the bush," Blondin-Andrew had a childhood typical of many Dene and Inuit Indians of her generation. She was born in Fort Norman, Northwest Territories, Canada, in 1951 to a young, unmarried mother, Cecilia Modeste. At three months of age Blondin-Andrew was adopted by her uncle and aunt, Joseph and Marie Therese (Tatti) Blondin, and raised with their children. The relative Blondin-Andrew credits most with shaping her determination to succeed in life, however, was her grandmother, Catherine Blondin.

Shaped by difficult early life

As a child Blondin-Andrew spent several happy years in the family's bush camp before being sent away to residential school in Inuvik at age nine. Three years later, when she was diagnosed with tuberculosis of the spine, she moved to a sanatorium in Edmonton, Alberta. After she recovered Blondin-Andrew returned to the family's new home, which they had purchased for $80, in the isolated community of Fort Franklin near Great Bear Lake. She later recalled that these years in a poorly heated house without electricity or running water, though difficult, made her stronger and gave her perspective.

At the age of 14 Blondin-Andrew was selected for leadership training and sent to Grandin College, a co-educational high school in Fort Smith. Her achievements there seemed threatened when, pregnant and unmarried at age 17, she was sent to a home for unwed mothers. Blondin-Andrew refused to give up her son. By age 21 she had married and was studying at the University of Alberta and raising three children, Troy, Tanya, and Tim Townsend. After graduating in 1974 with a bachelor's degree in education, Blondin-Andrew taught school in remote Native communities around the Northwest Territories for several years. She was appointed an aboriginal languages specialist for the Department of Education in Yellowknife. Her marriage ended in divorce.

Elected to parliament

Blondin-Andrew became a senior civil servant in the mid-1980s. At the national indigenous development program in Ottawa, which trained Natives for government jobs, she was appointed manager and then acting director of the public service commission. When the program ended, she returned to Yellowknife to become assistant deputy minister in the territorial government's Department of Culture and Communications. But Blondin-Andrew decided the best way to implement real change for her people was to run for elected office. Though politically inexperienced and poorly funded, Liberal party candidate Blondin-Andrew defeated her two male opponents by a landslide in the 1988 election, thus becoming the first Native woman elected to sit in the Canadian House of Commons.

After her election Blondin-Andrew became aboriginal affairs critic for the Liberal opposition government. During the Mohawk land dispute at Oka, Quebec, Blondin-Andrew earned widespread respect and media attention for her sharp questioning of Prime Minister Brian Mulroney. She also chaired her party's Western/Northern caucus and cochaired the leadership convention. When the Liberals were elected to office in 1993, Blondin-Andrew was given the junior cabinet post of secretary of state with responsibility for youth and training.

Continues activism

In August 1993 Blondin-Andrew married Leon Andrew, a Fort Norman trapper. Five months later, she charged her husband with two counts of spousal assault, stating that while she was sympathetic to her husband's problems, women could not allow themselves to be victimized. The couple reconciled while Andrew was serving his jail sentence. As a cabinet minister, Blondin-Andrew has continued working to legislate change for Canada's native peoples.

Where to learn more

Calgary Herald, January 13, 1991, p. A8.

Home Maker's, January/February, 1993, pp. 84-90.

O'Handley, Kathyrn, editor, *Canadian Parliamentary Guide,* Globe and Mail Publishing, 1994.

Simpson, Kieran, editor, *Canadian Who's Who,* University of Toronto Press, 1993.

Margaret Bourke-White

Born June 14, 1904
New York, New York

Died August 27, 1971
Stamford, Connecticut

American photojournalist

A photographer who captured historic events of the twentieth century

M argaret Bourke-White's name is synonymous with the photo essays that launched two of the great magazines published by Henry R. Luce, *Fortune* and *Life*. Through her photographs Bourke-White captured significant historical periods of the twentieth century, such as life in the Soviet Union, World War II (1939-1945), the independence of India from British rule, and apartheid (separation of races) in South Africa. Many of her photo assignments evolved into books with pictures that exposed poverty or discrimination. Bourke-White was fearless, often putting her life in danger to get just the right shot. Her black and white photographs came to be regarded as art rather than simply images accompanying a news story.

"In a whole lifetime of taking pictures a photographer knows that the time will come when he will take one picture that seems the most important of all. And you hope that everything will be right."

Father's influence

Bourke-White was born on June 14, 1904, in the Bronx, New York, the second of three children of Joseph and Minnie

White. When she was four the family moved to Bound Brook, New Jersey. Both of Bourke-White's parents influenced her life strongly, particularly her father. A designer and builder of large printing presses, Bourke-White's father maintained that machines were as beautiful as anything in nature. Often he would take Bourke-White to work with him so she could watch the presses in action. Exposure to these machines would later play a significant role in Bourke-White's career as an industrial photographer.

One fact Joseph White kept hidden for years from his children was that he was Jewish. Because he was fearful of anti-Semitism (discrimination against Jews), the Whites raised their children without a religion, even though Minnie White was Irish Catholic. Bourke-White kept her Jewish ancestry to herself, but she strongly identified with minorities, especially African Americans.

Studies photography

Bourke-White claimed never to have used a camera until after her father's death in January 1922, but her love for him and his own interest in photography was a strong incentive. After attending Columbia University in New York City for a year, she studied photography with photographer Clarence H. White, who believed photography was an art and each photograph had to be carefully planned. Having no money for college, Bourke-White received an offer from a wealthy patron who suggested she enroll in the University of Michigan in Ann Arbor, majoring in herpetology (the study of reptiles and amphibians). When one of her professors advised her to switch to a field she really liked, she chose photography. While Bourke-White was in college she married Everett Chapman, an engineering student. After living in Indiana and Ohio and attending a number of colleges, she left her husband and enrolled at Cornell University in Ithaca, New York. After graduation Bourke-White moved to Cleveland, Ohio, divorced her husband, and decided to hyphenate the last names of her mother and father as her new name, Bourke-White.

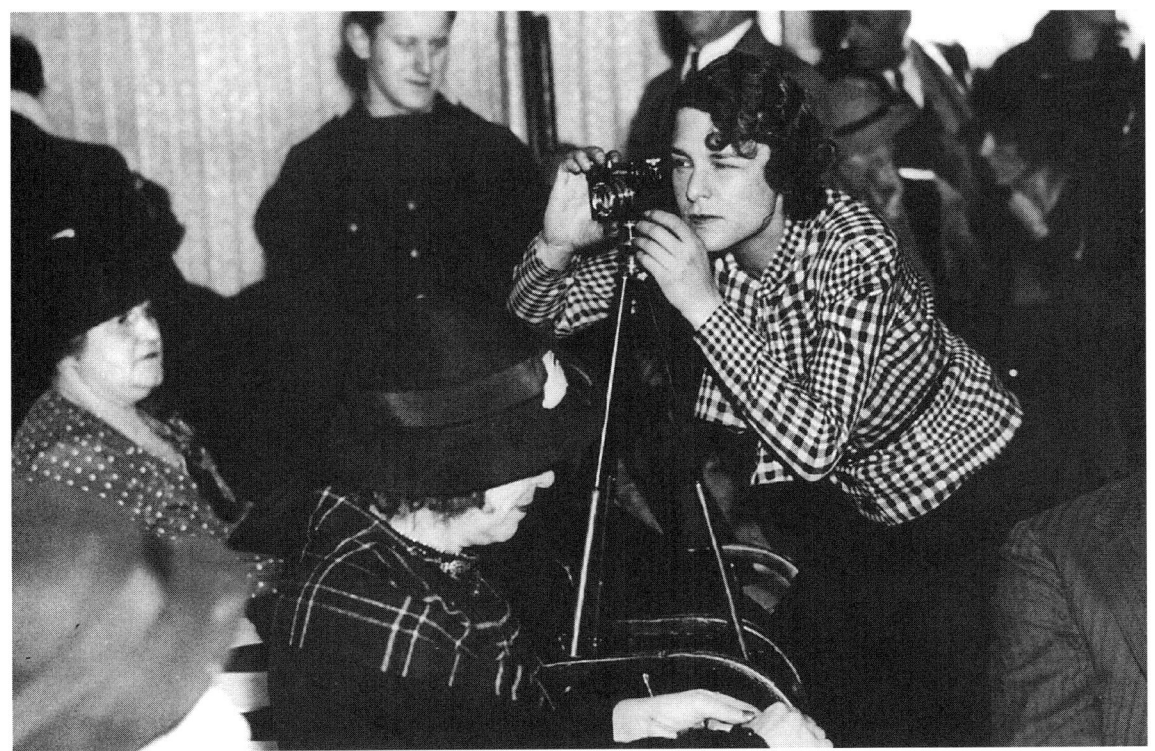

Perfects industrial photography

When Bourke-White entered the photography profession it was considered men's work, and throughout her career she often encountered resistance when she wanted to take a photograph. This was her experience when she was preparing for her now-famous photographs of steel mills in Cleveland. Only after a friend's intervention with the president of Otis Steel were the mills' gates opened to her. With Alfred Hall Bemis she photographed the mills at night, but the photographs did not turn out. Since this was a time before flash attachments, Bemis suggested using magnesium flares. The result was breathtaking photographs that ran in midwestern newspapers and led to Bourke-White's first book, *The Story of Steel,* an excellent example of industrial photography. Next came a telegram from Henry R. Luce, the publisher of *Time* magazine, who was starting a new business magazine called *Fortune.* He hired Bourke-White to take industrial photographs to illustrate the stories. The first issue, in February 1930, featured her photographs of the slaughtering process at the Swift meat-packing plant.

Revolutionizes photography

Despite the Great Depression, a period of severe economic crisis in the United States that lasted from 1929 until 1933, significant advances took place in photography and printing. The result was better-looking magazine photographs. At the center of this revolution was Bourke-White, who was always in pursuit of interesting photographs, even if this proved dangerous. Knowing the difficulty of taking photographs in Russia, Bourke-White nevertheless went there. After much resistance she photographed Soviet industry–the first non-Soviet to do so–and published her photographs in *Eyes over Russia.* During one of her other trips there, she was able to photograph Soviet leader Joseph Stalin. She also made a photographic record of the German air assault on Russia in 1939, just prior to World War II.

Life changed by Dust Bowl tragedy

During the 1930s Bourke-White worked half the year as an advertising photographer and the other half for *Fortune.* Her photographs of the devastation caused by a drought in the West, in the region called the Dust Bowl, focused national attention on the disaster that caused people to lose their farms and forced them to migrate to other parts of the country. This tragedy touched Bourke-White profoundly; she wrote, "I had never seen people caught helpless like this in total tragedy." She decided not to take advertising photographs anymore; instead, she would view her photos as "a great need to understand my fellow Americans better."

Marries Erskine Caldwell

Bourke-White's desire to photograph Americans led her to be teamed with Erskine Caldwell, the author of *Tobacco Road,* who wanted to write a book about southern sharecroppers.

Caldwell was quiet, even moody, like Bourke-White's father, but his way of getting a story from a person allowed Bourke-White to wait for the right moment to take a picture. The result was *You Have Seen Their Faces,* a milestone in photography. One book reviewer wrote, "The pictures have the quality of the very finest portraits. They depict man and the intention of his soul." Bourke-White married Caldwell on February 27, 1939. They traveled to Europe for their second book, *North of the Danube.* Their marriage lasted only five years because Bourke-White's career came between them, although they parted amicably.

Originates photo essay

When Luce founded *Life* he chose Bourke-White to be its chief photographer. In this pre-television age, Luce's goal was for the magazine "to eyewitness great events." Her first job was to photograph Fort Peck Dam on the Columbia River in Montana, which was a surrounded by a boom town named New Deal in honor of the economic program designed by President Franklin Roosevelt to help the country recover from the Great Depression. Taking pictures of the faces of workers, their children, and shanty-homes, Bourke-White introduced the photo essay story.

Makes more history

After the war Bourke-White continued to capture the great changes taking place in the world. She traveled to India to photograph Mohandas Gandhi, the nonviolent leader in the quest for India's independence from England. Her photograph

Photographs World War II

As the first female military photographer of World War II, Bourke-White frequently put her life in danger. Thinking she would be safer, the military put her on a ship, but it was it torpedoed by a German submarine. In Algiers, Algeria, Colonel Jimmy Doolittle agreed to take her up in the lead plane of a bomber mission to strike a German airfield in North Africa. Since the warplanes were not pressurized or heated, Bourke-White wore electric mittens as she figured out how to take photographs from 15,000 feet. Turning her attention to the ground soldier, Bourke-White photographed the fighting in the Cassino Valley of Italy. Her film was later lost in Washington, D.C., by the government. At the end of the war Bourke-White photographed corpses at the Nazi concentration camp at Buchenwald, documenting the worst horror of the twentieth century.

of Gandhi on his day of silence next to his spinning wheel is world-famous. In 1950 *Life* sent Bourke-White to South Africa, where she found blacks working in the diamond and gold mines under the worst possible conditions. Risking personal danger, Bourke-White descended two miles underground to photograph two men who were identified by numbers tattooed on their arms. During her coverage of the Korean War she looked for a story that pitted brother against brother. She found it in Nim Churl-In, who fought for the Communists but then returned home to apologize to his brother for his betrayal. Describing her feelings, Bourke-White said, "This time my heart was moved."

Suffers fatal disease

In 1951 Bourke-White experienced a strange feeling in her leg that spread through other parts of her body. After going to many doctors, she found one who said exercise was the best treatment for her. Eventually Bourke-White learned that she was suffering from Parkinson's disease, a progressive and fatal condition. In 1959 she underwent an operation that improved her health. During this time her friend, the great photographer Alfred Eisenstaedt, photographed her for a story in *Life* that informed the American public about her disability. A television special followed, and in 1963 Bourke-White wrote her autobiography, *Portrait of Myself*, which discussed her tragedy. She wrote that the disease was "one of the great experiences of my life. I would not be without it even if I had the power to wipe it out of my past." Bourke-White died on August 27, 1971, in Stamford, Connecticut.

Where to learn more

Ayer, Eleanor H., *Margaret Bourke-White: Photographing the World,* Dillon Press, 1992.

Bourke-White, Margaret, *Portrait of Myself,* Simon & Schuster, 1963.

Daffron, Carolyn, *Margaret Bourke-White,* Chelsea House, 1988.

Goldberg, Vicki, *Margaret Bourke-White,* Harper & Row, 1986.

McLenighan, Valjean, *Women Who Dared,* Raintree, 1979.

Silverman, Jonathan, *For the World to See: The Life of Margaret Bourke-White,* Viking, 1983.

Gwendolyn Brooks

Born June 7, 1917
Topeka, Kansas
African American poet
Pulitzer Prize-winning black
poet and poet laureate of
the Library of Congress

"Very early in life I became fascinated with the wonders language can achieve. And I began playing with words. That word-play is what I have been known for chiefly."

A leading contemporary American poet, the first black writer to be honored with a Pulitzer Prize, and the first black woman to be named poet laureate of the Library of Congress, Gwendolyn Brooks is acclaimed for her portraits of black urban life. Throughout a career that has spanned six decades and includes poetry and fiction, Brooks has been noted for her portraits of everyday life, in which she illuminates racism, poverty, interracial prejudice, and personal alienation.

Encouraged by parents and mentors

Brooks was born June 7, 1917, in Topeka, Kansas. When she was still an infant, her family moved to Chicago, where she still lives. Her path to becoming a writer started with her parents, who encouraged her to read and write. Her father, David, regularly told her stories and read aloud, while her mother, Keziah, a schoolteacher, composed songs for her children. As a young girl Brooks read widely and spent many hours composing rhymes and poems that she copied into a notebook.

When she was 13 Brooks published her first poem in the popular children's magazine *American Childhood.* Three years later she had the opportunity to show her work to James Weldon Johnson and Langston Hughes. Johnson and Hughes were two of the most famous poets of the 1920s black literary movement known as the Harlem Renaissance. They both assured her that she had talent and urged her to continue writing and studying poetry. While in high school Brooks regularly contributed poems to the *Defender,* a black daily newspaper in Chicago. After she graduated from Wilson Junior College in 1936 with a degree in English, she went to work for the National Association for the Advancement of Colored People Youth Council in Chicago. During this time she met Henry Lowington Blakely, whom she married in 1939. They have two children.

In 1941 Brooks's writing received another boost when she enrolled in a workshop led by Inez Cunningham Stark, a wealthy writer and scholar who traveled to the predominantly black South Side of Chicago to instruct aspiring poets. Brooks developed a local reputation with her poetry, and, in 1943, received a poetry award from the Midwestern Writers Conference. Soon thereafter her work would gain national attention.

Publishes nationally

Brooks submitted a manuscript of poems to Harper & Row, a New York publishing house, which published it as a book titled *A Street in Bronzeville.* Drawing from scenes and characters in her Chicago neighborhood and exploring prejudice, Brooks offered insight into the aspirations and struggles of ordinary black people. The poems received wide critical acclaim and Brooks was hailed as a major new voice in contemporary poetry. She received a Guggenheim Fellowship and was named by *Mademoiselle* as one of the magazine's "Ten Women of the Year." Her next book of poetry, *Annie Allen,* traces the coming of age of a black woman. It won the 1950 Pulitzer Prize, marking the first time the award had been bestowed upon a black writer.

Brooks during a 1989 ceremony in her honor.

Now established as a poet, Brooks ventured to write her first and only novel, *Maud Martha,* which was published in 1953. Like *Annie Allen,* the novel focuses on the life of a young black woman and, like Brooks's poetry, scrutinizes ordinary and everyday things to illuminate larger issues and themes. In her 1960 book of poems, *The Bean Eaters,* Brooks examined black social issues. Among them are the integration of the Little Rock, Arkansas, school system (see **Daisy Bates** entry), the lynching of blacks in the South, and the misguided efforts of cultured whites to help blacks. *The Bean Eaters* appeared just as the civil rights movement was gaining momentum, and with the book's political overtones, it received mixed reviews.

Political poetry

In 1967 Brooks attended a writers' conference at Fisk University in Nashville, Tennessee, and became acquainted with John Killens, Ron Milner, and LeRoi Jones, writers who were developing a new perspective for black authors. Their ideas influenced Brooks's next book, *In the Mecca,* which depicts problems of urban life and mentions contemporary black political heroes such as Malcolm X and Medgar Evers. At this point Brooks shifted focus in her writing by choosing a new publisher, Broadside Press. Her next three books, *Riot* (1969), *Family Pictures* (1970), and *Beckonings* (1975), also show a political emphasis; in them Brooks discussed revolution, black power, and black nationalism. At this point her style became almost totally free verse. Brooks explained these themes, which would continue to dominate her work: "What I'm fighting for now in my work, [is] for an expression relevant to all manner of blacks, poems I could take into a tavern, into the street, into the halls of a housing project. I don't want to say these poems have to be simple, but I want to clarify my language. I want these poems to be free. I want them to be direct without sacrificing the kinds of music, the picture making I've always been interested in."

Helps others

In addition to her own writing, Brooks is active in promoting and encouraging the work of other poets. In Illinois, where she was named poet laureate in 1968, Brooks has organized numerous poetry competitions, often offering prize money from her own funds. She has visited elementary schools, colleges, prisons, and drug rehabilitation centers, bringing people the art of poetry. In 1985, at the age of 68, she was appointed poet laureate and poetry consultant to the Library of Congress, becoming the first black woman to be named to the post. At age 72, Brooks received a Lifetime Achievement Award from the National Endowment for the Arts. In addition to the many other honors she has received in her distinguished career, the Gwendolyn Brooks Center for African American Literature was established at Western Illinois University, and a junior high school in Harvey, Illinois, was named after her.

Where to learn more

Brooks, Gwendolyn, *Report from Part One: An Autobiography,* Broadside Press, 1972.

Kent, George E., *A Life of Gwendolyn Brooks,* University Press of Kentucky, 1990.

Frances Hodgson Burnett

Born November 24, 1849
Manchester, England
Died October 29, 1924
Long Island, New York
British-born American author
Prolific writer of beloved
children's books

Frances (Eliza) Hodgson Burnett was a writer who won lasting acclaim for her children's books. She had insight into children's fears and desires and wrote compelling books that gained large reading audiences. She was able to use her own childhood experiences of hardship, upheaval, and insecurity in her fiction. Besides her classic children's books such as *A Little Princess*, *Little Lord Fauntleroy* and *The Secret Garden*, Burnett wrote realistic novels about adults, again using her own experience. The death of her teenage son turned her attention to writing about youthful death. Burnett was a flamboyant figure whose divorce caught the attention of society. She became a naturalized American citizen in 1905 and her books reflect both American and British themes and customs.

"[The success of my writing comes from] the way in which the most wildly romantic situation is made compatible with perfectly every-day and unromantic people and things."

Immigrates to America

Burnett was born on November 24, 1849, in Manchester, England, where her father operated a furniture store. He died when Burnett was only four years old, and in the ensuing few years her mother tried desperately to both maintain the family store and raise five children. But by 1865 Manchester's economy, which depended primarily on textiles, had become undone by the curtailing of American cotton exports during the Civil War (1861-1865). Burnett's mother was therefore compelled to sell the family business and leave the increasingly impoverished city. The family immigrated to the United States and settled near Knoxville, Tennessee, where Burnett's uncle lived. Life was still difficult, but for young Burnett, who had loathed Manchester's miserable weather and the grime from the mills, the open expanses and clear skies of her new home proved invigorating. By this time, Burnett–still in her mid-teens–had already begun writing stories for her own amusement, and when the family fortunes continued to stagnate, she began sending her stories to women's magazines. Throughout the 1860s she published stories in nearly every popular American magazine.

Moves to Paris

In 1871 Burnett made her first contribution to a more literary publication, *Scribner's Monthly*, and in 1873 she commenced serialization of her first novel, *Dolly: A Love Story*, in *Peterson's Ladies' Magazine*. By the early 1870s Burnett was sufficiently prosperous to finance a trip to her British homeland. Upon returning to the United States in 1873 she married a Tennessee doctor, Swan Burnett. The next year–after Burnett had given birth to Lionel, the first of their two children–the family moved to Paris, France, where Burnett's husband specialized in ophthalmology. In Paris the couple's fortunes diminished, though Burnett continued to publish in American magazines. In 1876, after Burnett had given birth to her second son, Vivian, the family returned to the United States and settled in Washington, D.C., where Burnett's husband established a medical practice.

Throughout the remainder of the 1870s and into the 1880s Burnett published several novels. Perhaps the most artistically successful of Burnett's adult novels is *Through One Administration* (1883), in which an unhappily married woman finds herself

Selected books by Frances Hodgson Burnett

Little Lord Fauntleroy **(1886)** Cedric Fauntleroy is guided by his seemingly infallible sense of fair play while living with his cold, aristocratic grandfather.

Editha's Burglar **(1888)** A little girl discovers a burglar and brings him her belongings so that he won't awaken her parents.

Giovanni and the Other Children Who Have Made Stories **(1892)** A collection of somber tales about dead or dying children.

Piccino, and Other Child Stories **(1894)** A pet kitten is puzzled by a young girl's apparent nap (she has actually died).

A Little Princess **(1905)** In this fairy tale Sara becomes a servant for a school's abusive headmistress when it is revealed that her father has died.

The Secret Garden **(1911)** An orphan named Mary lives in a vast old home that has a neglected garden. There she befriends two boys, Colin and Dick, and they begin tending the garden, which flourishes under their care and consideration, as do members of the household.

frustrated by conventions and expectations while circulating among high society in Washington, D.C. But not all of Burnett's adult novels are realistic fare; she also produced several cheery, whimsical works about social rags-to-riches achievement.

Starts writing children's stories

In 1879 Burnett, while already serializing novels and contributing short stories to various periodicals, also began publishing children's stories. Notable among these tales is *Editha's Burglar* (1888), in which a little girl discovers a burglar and brings him her belongings so that he doesn't awaken her parents.

Burnett's first major success in children's literature came when, in 1886, she published *Little Lord Fauntleroy*. This book concerns a little boy, Cedric Fauntleroy, who is guided

Movie Adaptations

Little Lord Fauntleroy **(1914)** The story of a fatherless American boy who discovers he's an heir to a British dukedom. This version stars **Mary Pickford** (see entry). Other versions were done in 1936, starring Mickey Rooney, and in 1980.

The Little Princess **(1939)** A young schoolgirl in Victorian London is sent to a harsh boarding school. While there her military father is reported missing in action and she must work as a servant to pay her keep. Stars **Shirley Temple** (see entry). Remade in 1987 and again in 1995.

The Secret Garden **(1949)** An orphaned girl arrives at her uncle's somber Victorian estate in England. She starts tending a long-forgotten garden, and with its resurrection, joy returns to the household. Remade several times–1984, 1987, 1993, and 1994 (animated).

by his seemingly infallible sense of fair play. Living with his cold, repulsive grandfather, an aristocrat, Fauntleroy risks losing his substantial inheritance rather than compromise his own exacting standards of democracy and fairness. In keeping to his own, admirable sense of fairness, Fauntleroy ultimately wins the love-and, thus, the promise of inherited fortune-of his crusty grandfather, who ultimately undergoes a humanizing transformation before his lovable grandson. With its heart-warming rendering of love and fortunes found, *Little Lord Fauntleroy* endeared itself to American and British readers. Burnett capitalized on the book's success by adapting it for the stage. This version also won great favor and redoubled the book's already substantial sales, thus making it one of the best-selling books at that time.

Son's death from tuberculosis

As Burnett's literary career continued to great acclaim, her personal life became increasingly anguished and unhappy; her marriage was unfulfilling, so Burnett separated from her husband. Then tragedy struck when her 15-year-old son

Actress **Mary Pickford**
(see entry) in the 1914
movie version of Little
Lord Fauntleroy

Lionel fell ill with tuberculosis. Throughout most of 1890 Burnett traversed Europe, Lionel in tow, hoping to find a sanitarium where her son could be assured of complete recovery. Unfortunately, Lionel never recovered.

After Lionel's death Burnett traveled to Italy, where she wrote *Giovanni and the Other Children Who Have Made Stories* (1892), a collection of somber tales about dead or dying children. Around this time Burnett also published a memoir, *The One I Knew the Best of All: A Memory in the Mind of a Child* (1893), in which she recounts her youthful enthusiasm for writing. In 1894 Burnett published another melancholy collection, *Piccino, and Other Child Stories.* This volume includes a particularly mawkish tale in which a pet kitten is puzzled by a young girl's apparent nap (she has actually died).

By the end of the nineteenth century Burnett was a somewhat notorious public figure. Though a prominent children's writer, she was also known for her flamboyant attire. In

1898 Burnett divorced her husband. Two years later, however, she became the target of gossip when she married her play-writing collaborator, Stephen Townesend, who was younger than Burnett by 10 years. This marriage, like the first, proved an unhappy one, and within three years the couple separated.

Wrote two big successes

In 1905 Burnett realized another literary success with *A Little Princess,* fashioning the story as a modern-day fairy tale. The main character, Sara, is received as a princess when she arrives at Miss Minchin's Seminary, but when it is revealed that her father has died destitute, Sara becomes a servant for the school's abusive headmistress. Her background is eventually uncovered by a wealthy recluse living nearby, and he enables her to recover her fortune and overcome her enemies. The book won widespread favor and remains one of Burnett's most prized works.

The Secret Garden, written in 1911, is about a cantankerous orphan, Mary, who lives in a vast old home replete with a neglected garden. There she befriends two boys, Colin and Dick, and they begin tending the garden, which flourishes under their care and consideration. Likewise, the children grow and become more prosperous as they learn to nurture and tend. *The Secret Garden* is widely considered Burnett's greatest work and a major contribution to children's literature.

In her later years Burnett lived comfortably at her Plandome estate on Long Island, where she indulged her interest in gardening. She died there on October 29, 1924.

Where to learn more

Burnett, Constance Buel, *Happily Ever After: A Portrait of Frances Hodgson Burnett,* Vanguard Press, 1965.

Carpenter, Angelica Shirley, *Frances Hodgson Burnett: Beyond the Secret Garden,* Lerner Publications, 1990.

James, Edward T., editor, *Notable American Women: Biographical Dictionary,* volume I, Belknap Press, 1975.

Thwaite, Ann, *Waiting for the Party: The Life of Frances Hodgson Burnett,* Scribner's, 1974.

Susan Butcher

Born December 26, 1954
Cambridge, Massachusetts
American dogsled driver (musher)
The first person to win three
consecutive Iditarod sled dog races

Susan Butcher is a four-time winner of the annual 1,159-mile Iditarod Trail Sled Dog Race from Anchorage to Nome, Alaska, which had been a male-dominated event until she began participating in 1978. Since then Butcher has entered the race each year, placing first in 1986, 1987, 1988, and 1990. One of only two people to win four Iditarods and the first to win three consecutive races, she held the Iditarod speed record until 1994. According to *Sports Illustrated*, observers of the sport consider Butcher to be "the finest long-distance dog racer ever and one of the greatest mushers of all time."

The term musher originated with the French-Canadian word *marcher* (mar-*shay*), which means "to march" or "to go." The command "mush" was used by early dogsled drivers to get their dogs to move forward, and eventually the term "musher" was applied to the drivers themselves.

"The wilderness is their [the dogs] domain. The dogs know more about it than I do, and I'm better off trusting their instincts."

Loves animals and nature

Butcher was born on December 26, 1954, in Cambridge, Massachusetts, a city in the Boston metropolitan area. She is the youngest of two daughters of Charles Butcher, chairman of a family-owned chemical company, and Agnes Butcher, a psychiatric social worker. Butcher's parents did not believe in making distinctions between the gender roles of boys and girls, so she and her sister Kate learned such skills as carpentry before they were teenagers. Having helped her father try to restore an old sailboat, Butcher enjoyed the experience so much that she applied to a boat-building school when she was 16. Her application was rejected, she later said, because of her gender, but she did not pursue the matter: "I just decided to learn it elsewhere and do it better than they ever thought it could be done." Although she did not become a boat builder, she would show similar determination to succeed against odds as a dogsled racer.

From an early age Butcher loved the outdoors and disliked cities. She also preferred to be alone. As an eight-year-old she wrote a school essay titled "I Hate the City," in which she described plans to tear down her family home and build a small log cabin that would provide more room for grass. During vacations to the ocean shore in Maine, Butcher played in the surf and spent most of her time with her dog, Cabee. Her parents expected her to become a veterinarian because, as her father commented, she was "more comfortable with animals than she was with people." While Butcher was in junior high school she learned that she had a mild case of dyslexia, a condition that affects one's ability to read. For that reason she received constant tutoring in English and, although she earned A's and B's in science and math at the Warehouse Cooperative School in Cambridge, she decided a pre-veterinary major in college would be too challenging.

Enters first race

Instead of going to college at age 17 Butcher moved to Boulder, Colorado, and became interested in dogsled racing, or mushing. After two years in Boulder she went to the University of Alaska in Fairbanks, Alaska, to work on a project to save the endangered musk ox. She also wanted to learn mushing, so she bought three dogs. Living in an isolated log cabin in the Wrangell Mountains outside Fairbanks, Butcher hunted for food and practiced mushing. In 1977 she moved with the musk ox project to Unalakleet, Alaska, where she met Joe Reddington, Sr., who 10 years earlier had originated the Last Great Race on Earth, better known as the Iditarod Trail Sled Dog Race. After hiring Butcher to train dogs at his kennel and observing her dedication to mushing, Reddington predicted she would become an Iditarod champion. In her first step toward that goal she entered the 1978 race and finished in 19th place.

Meets future husband

After participating in the 1979 Iditarod, Butcher made plans to move to Eureka, Alaska. Shortly before she left, in 1980, she met David Monson, a lawyer and sled racer who represented a dog food company. Thinking she had a sponsor for her next race, Butcher placed a large order for dog food. The sponsor subsequently withdrew and left her with the bill for $6,000. In order to pay off her debt Butcher took a job at a fish factory in Anchorage and slept in her car or at the homes of friends. Over the next two years she gave Monson $10 or $25 at a time until the bill was paid. Monson was so impressed with her conscientiousness that he asked her for a date. By 1985 they were married, and Monson was the full-time manager of Butcher's career. The couple made their home at Eureka, located 100 miles south of the Arctic Circle, where they built four one-room

Training for the Iditarod

When Butcher's dogs are old enough she begins a training schedule with an overhead wheel-like device called a dog walker, to which she hooks the dog for a 30-minute walk so she can check how the animal moves. In the fall, she harnesses the dogs to a vehicle with wheels so she and Monson can take them for trips that become increasingly longer as they gain confidence. She pairs a young dog with a more experienced dog for runs through forests on a variety of trails to prevent them from becoming bored. The dogs look forward to these outings and can hardly wait to be put in the harness. By December, when they are running 25 to 75 miles a day, Butcher begins picking 20 dogs for the Iditarod team.

Butcher crosses the finish line to victory during the 1990 Iditarod Sled Dog Race.

cabins and the 120 dog houses that comprise the Trail Breaker Kennels. Within a span of five years after her marriage, Butcher won four out of five Iditarods, setting the speed record of 11 days, 1 hour, 53 minutes, 23 seconds.

Devoted to her dogs

Since Butcher began racing in 1978 her life has been completely focused on breeding, raising, and training dogs. She has bonded with every dog born at her kennel–as many as 150 Alaskan Husky sled dogs live there at a time–first by assisting at their births, then by giving them names and nurturing them as they grow from puppies into adult dogs. Describing the dogs as her "best friends," Butcher interacts with them as one would with human beings, including congratulating a mother dog on the birth of a litter of puppies or commending a young dog for learning a new skill. She even recognizes each dog's individual voice or howl. Butcher's friends and associates say this close bonding accounts for the willingness of the dogs to work hard for her during a race, and it is the reason she wins so many races. She becomes especially close with her lead dogs. An example was Tekla, one of Butcher's three original dogs and her first lead dog, who participated in many races and died in 1991 at the age of 15. Others are Granite and Tolstoy, who were leaders in the 1988 Iditarod. Butcher's devotion to her dogs extends to the race. Usually thinking of their welfare before her own, she carefully watches each dog along the route, making sure they are rested, fed, and healthy.

Finds adventure on the trail

Butcher and her dogs have encountered adventure on the race trail. For instance, at the beginning of the 1982 Iditarod, when Butcher's sled careened into a tree, she was bruised and 15 dogs were injured. Shortly after they rejoined the race a severe snowstorm completely erased the trail, driving Butcher 10 miles off course. She and the dogs were stranded for 52 hours in 80-mile-per-hour winds and 30-foot snowdrifts. They still managed to finish second in that race. During the 1985 Iditarod, Butcher and her team were attacked by a pregnant moose that killed two dogs, injured 13, and hurt Butcher's shoulder. Although they were rescued by a fellow racer who shot the moose, Butcher dropped out of the race.

Receives recognition

Butcher has set records in other sled races such as the Norton Sound 250, the Kobuk 220, the Kusko 300, and the John Beargrease race. She has twice been named Women's Sports Foundation Professional Sportswoman of the Year, and in 1990 she, Monson, and Granite were guests of President George Bush at the White House. The 1994 Iditarod was Butcher's 14th race, but she did not place and her speed record was broken by Mark Buser at 10 days, 13 hours, and 2 minutes. While she was preparing for the race she said it would probably be her last because she wants to take time to have a family and start an animal research center in Eureka.

Where to learn more

Dolan, Ellen M., *Susan Butcher and the Iditarod Trail,* Walker and Co., 1993.

"Musher," *New Yorker,* October 5, 1987, pp. 34-35.

New York Times, March 6, 1994.

Steptoe, Sonja, "The Dogged Pursuit of Excellence," *Sports Illustrated,* February 11, 1991, pp. 190-194+.

Wadsworth, Ginger, *Susan Butcher: Sled Dog Racer,* Lerner Publications, 1994.

Kim Campbell

Born March 10, 1947
Port Alberni,
British Columbia, Canada

Canadian politician

First woman prime
minister of Canada

K im Campbell made history even before she served as the first woman prime minister of Canada by becoming the nation's first female justice minister and attorney general. Within only five years she rose from a seat in parliament to the highest office in the country. A role model for young women, she has often been compared with the former prime minister of Britain, **Margaret Thatcher** (see entry), both for her conservative politics and her outspokenness.

Early life

Campbell was born Avril Phaedra Campbell, the second of two daughters of George Campbell, a Canadian government official, and Phyllis Campbell, a homemaker and yacht crewwoman. Her mother chose the name Avril because it was French for April, the month she was supposed to have been born (however, she arrived before the due date, in March), and Phaedra from a character in a Greek tragedy. When Campbell

"If I'm going to speak fully and passionately about things, I'm going to run the risk [of offending people]. You're either going to blandify yourself so nothing you say will ever be taken out of context, or you insist that people be mature enough to take you as you really are."

was 10 her parents' marriage crumbled. Her mother left to pilot sailboats in Europe and the Caribbean, later saying she had felt trapped by the restrictive Canadian divorce laws of the day. She did not see her children again for a decade. Avril changed her name to Kim when she was 12. Her mother, who is now Phyllis Vroom, expressed little surprise at such an independent turn of mind in one so young. "I understand why she did it," she told the *Toronto Star.* "Kim suits her purposes much better." But Vroom also recognized her daughter's yearning for a more traditional home: "When I was in the West Indies, Kim sent me the family Bible–it was one of those pretty white Bibles with a zipper round it; my mother gave it to her–and asked me to fill in the family tree.... Kim was a vulnerable teenager, reaching out to her faraway mother."

Shows early leadership skills

At Prince of Wales secondary school in Vancouver, British Columbia, Campbell was elected school president, the first female president in the school's history. She told classmates that one day she wanted to be secretary-general of the United Nations. For her president's message in the school yearbook, she wrote, "Never afraid of new ideas, the students of Prince of Wales have shown that they can create new traditions while maintaining the old." She would use basically the same theme in Tory (conservative) politics more than 25 years later. Campbell enrolled at the University of British Columbia, where she was elected freshman president and also met her future husband, mathematics professor Nathan Divinsky, who was 22 years her senior. They married in 1972 but then divorced in 1982. After graduating with honors in political science Campbell won a four-year Canada Council fellowship to the London School of Economics in London, England.

Enters politics

Upon her return from London in 1980 Campbell enrolled in law school at the University of British Columbia in Vancouver. That year she also won election to a seat on the Vancouver school board. School board debates often became heated, and Campbell soon earned a reputation as a fighter. She also made enemies. After completing law school she joined the prestigious Vancouver law firm of Ladner Downs. Seeking the leadership post of the provincial Social Credit Party ("Socred") in 1986, she finished last in a field of 12 candidates. But during an impassioned speech for the post at a party gathering, she criticized the eventual winner with the memorable line: "Charisma without substance is a dangerous thing." That observation helped create her image as a colorful figure, but opponents would later apply the same criticism to Campbell as she sought higher offices.

In 1986 she won a seat in the provincial government, then another in the national House of Commons two years later after a close race. Her support of the North American Free Trade Agreement (NAFTA), a treaty that removed trade barriers among countries on the North American continent–Canada, the United States, and Mexico–was appreciated by then Prime Minister Brian Mulroney. In 1990, only seven years after Campbell earned her law degree, he appointed her justice minister and attorney general, then named her defense minister.

Becomes prime minister

Campbell made the most of her high-profile posts. Nevertheless she continued to speak her mind, once making a comment that many considered blatantly anti-Catholic and thus offensive in a country with a large Catholic population. Yet she was able to capitalize on her charisma and popularity, especially among young women, and she cultivated ties with all social classes. She told an interviewer, "As an intellectually oriented person, I like to socialize with people who read the same things as I do ([novelists] Dostoyevsky, Tolstoy, Jane Austen) and have a similar level of education, but I genuinely like ordinary people." She also claimed that beneath her "cool, arrogant, intellectual, urbane exterior" there "beats the heart of a Texas line dancer." An accomplished cello player, she speaks three languages: English, Russian, and French.

By the time Mulroney left office in June 1993 with the lowest popularity rating of any Canadian leader in the twentieth century, Campbell was ready to take his place. At the Progressive Conservative Party convention, having acquired the support of more delegates than all five of her male opponents, she became Mulroney's successor and the first woman prime minister of Canada. During her first weeks in office she carried out a campaign pledge to decrease the size and cost of government by eliminating 15 cabinet positions and convincing her ministers to ride taxis instead of chauffeured cars to work. She was also a major participant in an international trade summit in Tokyo, Japan. When general elections were held the following October, however, Campbell was voted out of office as the Liberal Party defeated the conservatives throughout the country. At the end of the year she resigned her post as Conservative Party leader, returning to private life as a lecturer in government at a Canadian university and a commentator on public affairs for news organizations.

Where to learn more

Newsweek, June 14, 1993.

New York Times, June 20, 1993; June 26, 1993; October 26, 1993; December 14, 1993.

Toronto Star, May 1, 1993.

Luisa Capetillo

Born October 28, 1879
Arecibo, Puerto Rico

Died April 10, 1922
Rio Piedras, Puerto Rico

Puerto Rican feminist

Leader of political and labor
struggles in Puerto Rico

"Capetillo was a tireless feminist who battled a culture that denied women educational opportunities, career choices, and economic advancement."

Luisa Capetillo–remembered as the first woman to wear pants–was a feminist and labor rights activist in Puerto Rico in the early 1900s. She tirelessly battled for women to have educational opportunities, career choices, and economic advancement. Capetillo criticized her society for forcing girls into marriages based not on love but on a financial agreement between parents. Many of her ideas were far ahead of her time, and, until recently, she was overlooked as an important historical figure.

Wears pants in public

Capetillo was born on October 28, 1879, in Arecibo, Puerto Rico. Her mother, Margarita Peron, was French, and her father, Luis Capetillo, was Spanish. She may have had some formal schooling, but she was mostly self-taught. Because she had learned French from her mother, she was able to study the works of French writers on her own. Achieving knowledge this way probably led to the growth of Capetillo's independent spirit in adulthood. History remembers her as the first woman to wear pants–instead of skirts or dresses–in public. Dressing in pants like the men of the time was a symbolic statement of Capetillo's personal freedom.

Fights for workers' rights

Capetillo lived in the period when industry was just beginning to develop in Puerto Rico. Although wages for men were extremely low in the late 1800s and early 1900s, women's earnings were even lower. Capetillo believed that fair pay was a worker's right, regardless of gender. She felt that better wages for everyone would result in happier families, less domestic violence, and more educational opportunities for children. Capetillo's main concern lay with the plight of working women. In 1911 she wrote the book *Mi opinión sobre las libertades, derechos y deberes de la mujer como compañera, madre y ser independiente* (*My Opinion on the Freedom, Rights, and Duties of the Woman as Companion, Mother, and as an Independent Woman*). In this book she examined the vast differences between the lives of wealthy women and working women in the early 1900s. Having no obligation to take jobs outside the home to help support their families, well-to-do mothers had the financial resources to hire other women to look after their children. Capetillo's book makes clear that working women in the early 1900s did not have these luxuries but, rather, were victims of substandard economic and social conditions.

Arrested for union activities

Capetillo first became involved in the labor movement in 1907, when she took part in a strike in the Arecibo tobacco factories. Active in the local union, the Federation of Free Workers, she served as a reporter for the union's newspaper. To bring attention to women's issues she founded her own newspaper, *La Mujer* (*The Woman*), three years later. During the next few years Capetillo traveled extensively, promoting workers rights and journeying to New York to write articles for a newspaper called *Cultura obrera* (*Workers' Culture*). She also met with union leaders in Florida. From 1914 to 1916 she lived

The cooperative movement

A cooperative is a group that combines its members' money or talents to buy things or to accomplish specific goals. The cooperative movement began in Great Britain in the 1800s and rapidly spread throughout the world. An international alliance was formed in 1895. The concept of sharing goods and services in a network led to the formation of cooperatives in agriculture, manufacturing, insurance, medical services, and housing. Many of these organizations still exist. For instance, the modern credit union is a result of the cooperative movement.

in Cuba, teaching workers how to start cooperatives (organizations owned by those using the organizations' services). Returning to Puerto Rico in 1918, she immediately became involved in organizing strikes by farm workers. Because activist agitation by women was considered shocking at that time, she was arrested for violence, disobedience, and being disrespectful to a police officer.

Writes about better future

Capetillo left behind many written works that are just now being rediscovered and studied. Dedicated to all workers, her essays and books reveal her dreams of a better world in the future. In *La Humanidad en el futuro* (*Humanity in the Future*), published in 1910, she writes about a utopian society (a perfect society governed by ideal laws), the power of the church and the state, private and public property, and marriage. Capetillo also wrote several dramas. The theater gave her a chance to creatively and publicly express her radical opinions about the social oppression of women. Capetillo died of tuberculosis on April 10, 1922, at the age of 42. She was survived by her three children, her feminist writings, and her hopes for a better world.

Where to learn more

Capetillo, Luisa, *Mi opinión sobre las libertades, derechos y deberes de la mujer como compañera, madre y ser independiente* (*My Opinion on the Freedom, Rights, and Duties of the Woman as Companion, Mother, and as an Independent Woman*), Tomes Publishing, 1911.

López Antonetty, Evelina, *Luisa Capetillo,* Centro de Estudios Puertorriqueños (Hunter College), 1986.

Valle Ferrer, Norma, *Luisa Capetillo: Historia de una mujer proscrita* (*Luisa Capetillo: History of an Exiled Woman*), Editorial Cultural, 1990.

Rachel Carson

Born May 27, 1907
Springdale, Pennsylvania

Died April 14, 1964
Silver Spring, Maryland

American marine biologist

Wrote Silent Spring, a
best-selling book on pesticides
that succeeded in banning DDT use

During the late 1940s and throughout the 1950s, worldwide use of chemical pesticides on crops and in pest control programs grew rapidly. The most popular pesticide was DDT, which had been promoted as the "savior of mankind" after it had been used successfully against typhus epidemics (widespread disease transmitted by body lice) in Italy and was proven to be effective in killing insects. The fact that DDT and several other widely used chemicals were highly toxic was not widely known, and they were highly promoted by the petrochemical (chemicals made from petroleum or natural gas) and agricultural industries. However, Rachel Carson, the National Book Award-winning author of environmental best-sellers, had researched DDT and discovered the threat it posed to the environment. Her book *Silent Spring* unleashed a heated controversy and led to the banning of DDT and other toxic chemicals. President Jimmy Carter recognized her service to environmental and human health in 1980 when he posthumously awarded her the President's Medal of Freedom.

"I can remember no time when I wasn't interested in the out-of-doors and the whole world of nature."

Early Life

The youngest of three children, Rachel Carson grew up in Springdale, Pennsylvania, a small town 20 miles north of Pittsburgh. Her parents, Robert Warden and Maria McLean Carson, lived on a farm and kept cows, chickens, and horses. The surrounding countryside, near the shores of the Allegheny River, was where Carson first learned about water, land, and animals. Her mother was the daughter of a Presbyterian minister and instilled in her own daughter a love of nature, music, art, and literature. A solitary child, Carson had few friends besides her cats, and she spent most of her time reading and studying nature. She began writing poetry at age eight and published her first story, "A Battle in the Clouds," in *St. Nicholas* magazine two years later. She claimed that her professional writing career began when *St. Nicholas* paid her a little over three dollars for one of her essays.

Pursues science career

In 1925 Carson received a scholarship from the Pennsylvania College for Women (now Chatham College) in Pittsburgh. Her freshman biology course had a major influence on her thinking, leading her to change her major from English to zoology in the middle of her junior year. After Carson graduated with high honors in 1928, her biology teacher helped her obtain a summer fellowship at the Marine Biology Laboratory at Woods Hole, Massachusetts. There she saw the ocean for the first time and encountered her first exotic sea creatures, including sea anemones and sea urchins. She received a scholarship from the Johns Hopkins University in Baltimore, Maryland, to study zoology and genetics, and she wrote her master's thesis on the embryonic and early larval life of the catfish. She graduated in June 1932.

Writes for the government

Because of the Great Depression, a period of worldwide economic crisis in the 1930s, jobs were not plentiful in 1932. Carson taught zoology at two universities in Maryland, but the salary was too little to live on. Her parents sold their home and moved to Maryland to ease some of their daughter's financial burdens. Then, in 1935, when her father died and left her with the responsibility of supporting her mother, Carson applied for a job at the Bureau of Fisheries. Although women were discouraged from taking the required civil service exam, Carson did well on the test and outscored all the other applicants. She was the second woman ever hired by the bureau for a permanent professional post.

Carson wrote and edited government publications at the Bureau of Fisheries and earned a reputation as a ruthless editor who would not tolerate poor writing. She submitted an essay to the *Atlantic Monthly* and, to her surprise, it was published as "Undersea" in 1937. That same year her older sister, Marian, died at the age of 40, and Carson then raised her nieces. "Undersea" was later expanded into the book *Under the Sea-Wind.* Despite favorable reviews, it sold fewer than 1,600 copies after six years in print. The book did, however, bring Carson to the attention of William Beebe, the American naturalist and explorer, who included an excerpt from Carson's book in his *Book of Naturalists.*

The Bureau of Fisheries was merged with the Biological Survey in 1940 and renamed the Fish and Wildlife Service. Carson quickly moved up in the professional ranks, eventually reaching the position of biologist and chief editor. She wrote a small book about national wildlife refuges, *Conservation in Action,* that took her back into the field. As part of her research she visited the Florida Everglades, Parker River in Massachusetts, and Chincoteague Island in Chesapeake Bay.

Becomes successful writer

Then Carson began work on a new book that focused on oceanography. She could now use previously classified government research data on oceanography, which included a number of technical and scientific breakthroughs. During the summer of 1949 Carson did undersea diving off the Florida coast. Then she battled skeptical administrators to arrange a deep-sea cruise to Georges Bank near Nova Scotia aboard the Fish and Wildlife

Service research vessel *Albatross III*. Her book on oceanography, *The Sea Around Us,* was published in 1951, becoming an unexpected success and remaining on the *New York Times* bestseller list for 86 weeks. As a result Carson won the National Book Award and several other honors. She retired from government service and devoted her time to writing.

Carson began work on another book, focusing this time on life along the shoreline. She took excursions to the coasts of Florida and returned to one of her favorite locations, the rocky shores of Maine. She fell in love with the Maine coast and in 1953 bought a summer home in West Southport on Sheepscot Bay. Her next book, *The Edge of the Sea,* appeared in 1955, earning more awards. The book stayed on the bestseller list for 20 weeks. RKO Studios bought the film rights, but the movie version sensationalized the material and ignored scientific fact. Carson corrected some of the more serious errors but considered the film embarrassing, even after it won an Oscar as the best documentary of 1953. In 1956 she published "Help Your Child Wonder" based on her childhood experiences. After her death, the essay reappeared in 1965 as the book *The Sense of Wonder.*

Investigates pesticide use

In 1956 one of Carson's nieces died, leaving her son in Carson's care. After legally adopting the boy that same year, she built a new winter home in Silver Spring, Maryland. Carson's next book grew out of a long-held concern about the overuse of pesticides. She had received a letter from Olga Owens Huckins, who described how aerial spraying of the toxic pesticide DDT had destroyed her bird sanctuary in Massachusetts. Carson thought the most effective tactic to stop the use of DDT would be to write an article for a popular magazine, but she decided to write a book instead.

Consulting with biologists, chemists, entomologists (scientists who study insects), and pathologists (specialists who interpret and diagnose the changes caused by disease in tissues and body fluids), Carson spent four years gathering data for her book, which she titled *Silent Spring.* When an excerpt

of the book first appeared in the *New Yorker* in June 1962, it drew a hostile response from the chemical industry. Carson argued that pesticide use upset nature's delicate balance. Although her message is no longer controversial, the book caused near panic in some circles. Chemical companies tried unsuccessfully to pressure the publisher, Houghton Mifflin, to suppress the book.

Carson appearing before the Ribicoff Committee in 1963.

Raises environmental awareness

Silent Spring soon attracted a large, concerned audience in America and around the world. A 1963 special CBS television broadcast, "The Silent Spring of Rachel Carson," featured a debate between Carson and a chemical company representative. Her cool-headed approach won her many fans and brought national attention to the problems associated with pesticide use. Although Carson's poor health prevented her from giving speeches, she did appear before the Ribicoff Commit-

Selected works by Rachel Carson

Under the Sea-Wind **(1941)** Carson describes sealife, focusing on three areas: the seashore, the sea itself, and the bottom of the sea.

The Sea Around Us **(1951)** Carson explains the processes that formed the earth, moon, and oceans in addition to discussing the factors that regulate climate.

The Edge of the Sea **(1955)** Carson interprets the community of plants and animals on the Atlantic coast of the United States "in terms of the essential unity that binds life to the earth."

Silent Spring **(1962)** An exposé of the damage done to the environment by the use of chemical pesticides, this book helped start the environmental movement.

The Sense of Wonder **(1965)** In a narrative accompanied by beautiful color photographs, Carson shows how adults and children can rediscover nature.

tee, the U.S. Senate committee on environmental hazards. In 1963 she received numerous honors, including an award from the Izaak Walton League of America, the Audubon Medal, and the Cullen Medal of the American Geographical Society. She was also elected to the American Academy of Arts and Sciences. Carson died of heart failure on April 14, 1964, at the age of 56. In 1980 President Jimmy Carter posthumously awarded her the President's Medal of Freedom.

Where to learn more

Foster, Leila Merrell, *The Story of Rachel Carson and the Environmental Movement,* Childrens Press, 1990.

Greene, Carol, *Rachel Carson: Friend of Nature,* Childrens Press, 1992.

Hendricksson, John, *Rachel Carson: The Environmental Movement,* Millbrook Press, 1991.

McKay, Mary A., *Rachel Carson,* Twayne Publishers, 1993.

Wadsworth, Ginger, *Rachel Carson: Voice of the Earth,* Lerner Publications, 1992.

Willa Cather

Born December 7, 1873
Back Creek Valley, Virginia

Died April 24, 1947
New York, New York

American writer

Wrote novels about the final phase of frontier life in the American West and won the Pulitzer Prize in literature

Although Willa Cather wrote relatively few novels, her work continues to be read today for its engrossing stories about pioneers and immigrants who settled the Western frontier. She captured a pivotal time in the nation's history, just before real estate developers moved into the West, when it was still possible for Americans to conquer their environment and pursue success on the land through toil and perseverence.

Cather was born Wilella Cather on December 7, 1873, in Back Creek Valley, Virginia, the oldest of seven children of Charles Fectique Cather, a farmer, and his wife Mary Virginia (Boak) Cather. As a child she was nicknamed "Willie," but later she changed her name to Willa after both her grandfathers, who were named William. In her early years as a writer she also adopted the name Seibert from her maternal grandmother, changing the spelling to Sibert. It was not until later that she became known as Willa Cather, the name that is widely famous today.

"Years from eight to fifteen are the formative period in a writer's life, when he consciously gathers basic material. He may acquire a great many interesting and vivid impressions in his mature years but his thematic material he acquires under fifteen years of age."

Moves to frontier

Cather spent her childhood at Willowshade, the family farm. The area surrounding Willowshade was a virtual paradise, and Cather spent her early years enjoying the freedom of the outdoors. However, in 1883, when she was nine, the family moved to a town called Red Cloud, Nebraska, where her father gave up farming for business. The quaint orderliness of farm life was replaced by the great expanse of the Western frontier. Cather was uprooted, but she shared her feelings of displacement with other frontier settlers such as Swedes, Bohemians, Germans, Poles, and Russians. The experience of moving so far from her childhood home made Cather deeply resentful of change. As a result she became a traditionalist, adhering only to tried-and-true customs and habits.

Wants to be a doctor

Although Cather finally started attending school in Red Cloud, much of her education took place outside of a formal setting. Until the age of nine she was primarily educated at home by her grandmother Seibert, who taught her the classical authors. She read *Pilgrim's Progress* by the eighteenth-century British writer John Bunyan, which became one of her favorite books. In Red Cloud she was influenced by the neighboring cultures of the French and Bohemian settlers through the friendships she made with foreign girls her own age. In high school she became interested in the theories of Charles Darwin, the nineteenth-century British naturalist who originated the theory of evolution. At an early age she decided to become not a writer, but a doctor. As she said later in life, "I didn't want to be an author. I wanted to be a surgeon! Thank goodness, I had a youth uncorrupted by literary ambitions.... I think it's too bad for a child to feel that it must be a writer, for then instead of looking at life naturally, it is hunting for cheap effects."

Becomes journalist

When Cather attended college in 1891 at the University of Nebraska she began her career as a writer. She excelled at

Selected novels by Willa Cather

O Pioneers! **(1913)** On the death of her father, Alexandra Bergson takes over the care of her family and the management of the farm, becoming deeply devoted to the land.

My Antonia **(1918)** Antonia Shimerda, a Bohemian immigrant, is forced to work as a servant on the farm of her neighbors after her father kills himself in despair at his failure to become a successful farmer.

One of Ours **(1922)** Claude Wheeler, a boy who grows up on a western farm, goes to a western university, enters the army, and is later killed in France.

A Lost Lady **(1923)** An aging beauty doomed to small-town life continues to dream of happier days when she gave hospitality to railroad builders.

The Professor's House **(1925)** Godfrey St. Peter, a middle-aged professor, is victimized by his wife's ambition and his daughter's desire for a higher social position.

Death Comes for the Archbishop **(1927)** Father Jean Marie Latour travels from the French Canadian provinces to Santa Fe, New Mexico, and realizes his lifelong ambition of building a cathedral. (Based on the true story of Jean Baptiste Lamy, the first archbishop of Santa Fe.)

journalism and short story writing, and even had her first story published in a Boston magazine. It was this event that made her decide to choose writing over science. As Cather said of her new obsession, "But what youthful vanity can be unaffected by the sight of itself in print! It has a kind of hypnotic effect." From this point on she devoted herself to writing. She began writing for the Lincoln, Nebraska, newspaper after she graduated in 1895. She moved to Pittsburgh, Pennsylvania, working first for a magazine called *Home Monthly* as an editor, then for a newspaper called the *Pittsburgh Daily Leader* as a copy editor and a music and drama critic. Cather gave up news writing for teaching in 1901 because she became exhausted by the life of a journalist.

Publishes first novel

During the time she spent teaching, Cather met Isabelle McClung, daughter of a prominent Pittsburgh judge. McClung granted Cather a patronage under which she wrote her first important tales and poems. She also accompanied Cather on her first trip to Europe in 1902. Afterward Cather published two works: a volume of verse titled *April Twilights* in 1903, and a book of tales, *The Troll Garden,* in 1905. These two works got the attention of S. S. McClure, publisher of *McClure's* magazine in New York, who gave Cather a job as managing editor. Not only had Cather returned to journalism, but she also became part of the up-and-coming literary world that was beginning to take root in Greenwich Village in New York at the time. However, in 1912, after publishing her first novel, *Alexander's Masquerade,* in serial form for *McClure's,* she resigned from the magazine and spent the rest of her life writing fiction.

From My Antonia *by Willa Cather. Illustrated by W.T. Benda.*

Wins Pulitzer Prize

After the publication of *Alexander's Masquerade,* which established the basic themes of her novels about the frontier, Cather wrote several books that established her as an important novelist. She enjoyed her first literary success with *O Pioneers!* (1913). Having grown up in Nebraska among immigrant farmers, she based this novel and subsequent works on the farm and prairie scenes of her childhood. Perhaps best known for *My Antonia* (1918), *The Professor's House* (1925), and *Death Comes for the Archbishop* (1927), Cather became recognized as a stoic, moral writer who did not forsake traditional values while writing in an age of changing standards. In 1922 she won the Pulitzer Prize for *One of Ours,* which is among her lesser-known works.

Movie Adaptations

Paul's Case **(1980)** An ambitious young man enters the upper crust of New York society through deceiving pretenses.

O Pioneers! **(1991)** An unmarried woman inherits her father's Nebraska homestead. Although the family has prospered through her investments, her brothers come to resent her influence.

My Antonia **(1995)** A young woman is forced to work on her neighbor's farm after her father commits suicide. Made by the USA television network.

Finds new themes

Cather spent her final years in an apartment on Park Avenue in New York City detached from the new literary world, forming friendships with prominent artists and musicians. Her last two novels, *Lucy Gayheart* (1935) and *Sapphira and the Slave Girl* (1940), continued her shift away from prairie themes to other subjects that had begun with the publication of *Death Comes for the Archbishop*. Cather also wrote a collection of tales titled *Obscure Destinies* (1932) and *Not Under Forty* (1936), essays addressed specifically to the older generation whose values the younger generation would not understand. In addition to receiving the Pulitzer Prize and many honorary degrees, Cather was awarded the Howells Medal of the American Academy of Arts and Letters in 1930 and the National Institute of Arts and Letters gold medal for fiction in 1944. She died in New York City at the age of 73 and was buried in Jaffrey, New Hampshire, a town where she had enjoyed autumn writing retreats.

Where to learn more

Robinson, Phyllis C., *Willa: The Life of Willa Cather,* Doubleday, 1983.

Keene, Ann T., *Willa Cather,* Julian Messner, 1994.

Shirley Chisholm

Born November 30, 1924
Brooklyn, New York

African American politician

First African American woman to be elected to Congress and to receive a major party presidential nomination

"That I am a national figure because I was the first person in 192 years to be at once a congressman, black and a woman proves, I think, that our society is not yet either just or free."

O utspoken and principled, Shirley Chisholm wanted nothing to do with the New York City political machine. She fought her way to victory to become the first African American congresswoman the hard way, thus earning her nickname, "Fighting Shirley Chisholm." Considered a maverick and a dissenter throughout her political career, Chisholm realized that "if you decide to operate on the basis of your conscience, rather than your political advantage, you must be ready for the consequences and not complain when you suffer them. There is little place in the political scheme of things for an independent, creative personality, for a fighter. Anyone who takes that role must pay a price."

Early life

Chisholm was born Shirley Anita St. Hill November 30, 1924, in Brooklyn, New York. Her early schooling took place on the Caribbean island of Barbados, where she and her two sisters were sent to live with their grandmother so her parents could save money for their children's education. "Years later I would know what an important gift my parents had given me by seeing to it that I had my early education in the strict, traditional, British-style schools of Barbados," Chisholm wrote in her autobiography. "If I speak and write easily now, that early education is the main reason." In 1934 she and her sisters rejoined their parents. Chisholm's father, a factory worker, introduced the youngsters to the teachings of African American nationalist leader Marcus Garvey. Her mother, Ruby Seale St. Hill, was a seamstress and domestic worker who "was thoroughly British in her ideas, her manners, and her plans for her daughters," Chisholm said. "We were to become young ladies–poised, modest, accomplished, educated, and graceful, prepared to take our places in the world." Since Chisholm's parents were strict, they did not allow much socializing and the girls attended church three times each Sunday.

Becomes teacher and politician

After graduating from high school, Chisholm enrolled at Brooklyn College, where she found a much bigger world than what her parents had allowed her to experience. She wanted to involve herself in something that would stop white mistreatment of blacks. Realizing political action was not open to a black woman, she saw teaching as the only way to reach her goal. After graduation she worked for seven years as a teacher at a nursery school in New York City. At the same time she pursued her master's degree in early childhood education at Columbia University, where she met Conrad Q. Chisholm. They were married on October 8, 1949.

During the years she worked in New York City, Chisholm gained a reputation as a political agitator. She recognized that the political clubs were dominated by men who kept political power to themselves and only allowed women to raise money. As she commented in her autobiography, "Of my two 'handicaps,' being female put many more obstacles in my path than being black."

In 1960 Chisholm helped form the Unity Democratic Club, an organization founded to promote and elect candidates for New York State's 17th Assembly district. Deciding to run herself, she won by a landslide victory in the 1964 election. Chisholm's success came largely from her ability to relate to people. For instance, she spoke Spanish in Puerto Rican neighborhoods and went directly to the women she would represent. Chisholm served on the New York legislature for the next four years, gaining a reputation as an effective lawmaker. She helped introduce bills to assist disadvantaged students and to grant unemployment insurance to domestic employees.

A change in the status quo

By the late 1960s the civil rights movement had sensitized the entire nation to the existence of racial discrimination. Changes in state and national laws gave redress to claims that inequality prevented many Americans from sharing in the promise of democracy. The women's movement followed on the heels of the civil rights movement, expanding the notion that equal rights meant equal rights for all Americans, without regard to gender or race.

Changes in the nation's political will enabled a number of black men to get elected to the U.S. Congress–the most since the period of Reconstruction after the Civil War, when 14 were elected to the U.S. House of Representatives, and two were elected to the U.S. Senate. But no black woman had ever been given a national mandate.

Wins congressional seat

Following the announcement of a redistricting plan for Brooklyn that would give minority areas an equal vote, Chisholm declared her candidacy for the 1968 elections. With few funds she entered a heated primary race against a much favored Democratic party candidate. Her hard work, combined with a low voter turnout, resulted in a slim primary victory. In the fall campaign she defeated the nationally known

civil rights leader James Farmer. Her campaign slogan was "Fighting Shirley Chisholm: Unbought and Unbossed." When she went to Washington she appointed women to her staff and dutifully helped constituents.

Chisholm proved to be a determined representative who was vocal in her support of programs and policies that benefited disadvantaged groups. She was criticized for not making

Presidential candidate

Chisholm was the first African American, as well as the first woman, to seek a major political party's nomination for the presidency. Chisholm's unsuccessful 1972 campaign for the presidency was more symbolic than realistic and was intended to prove a point. "I ran because someone had to do it first," she wrote in her book *The Good Fight.* "In this country everybody is supposed to be able to run for president, but that's never been really true. I ran because most people think the country is not ready for a black candidate, not ready for a woman candidate." Chisholm stayed in the race all the way to the Democratic National Convention with the hope that her candidacy would make it easier for future candidates who were not white males. During the final convention tally, Chisholm received a total of 151 votes.

political alliances and for not being willing to play the day-to-day game of political compromise. But she saw her duty differently, explaining: "I do not see myself as a lawmaker, an innovator in the field of legislation. America has the laws and the material resources it takes to insure justice for all its people. What it lacks is the heart, the humanity, the Christian love that it would take. It is perhaps unrealistic to hope that I can help give this nation any of those things, but that is what I believe I have to try to do." As a matter of conscience, Chisholm spoke out against the Vietnam War in her first congressional speech, saying she would vote against every military appropriations bill while in Congress. During her terms in office (1969-1982) she served on the Veterans Affairs Committee, the Education and Labor Committee, and the influential House Rules Committee. In 1972 she ran an unsuccessful campaign for the Democratic presidential nomination.

Retires from politics

Chisholm retired from public office in 1982 in order to spend more time with Arthur Hardwick, her second husband. She has taught politics at Mt. Holyoke College in Massachusetts. In 1984 she cofounded the National Political Congress of Black Women, which in 1988 sent a delegation of over 100 women to the Democratic National Convention. Chisholm also participated in the presidential campaigns of African American candidate Jesse Jackson, giving this reason for her support: "Jackson is the voice of the poor, the disenchanted, the disillusioned, and that is exactly what I was."

Where to learn more

Chisholm, Shirley, *The Good Fight,* Houghton Mifflin, 1973.

Chisholm, Shirley, *Unbought and Unbossed,* Houghton Mifflin, 1970.

Hicks, Nancy, *The Honorable Shirley Chisholm, Congresswoman from Brooklyn,* Lion Books, 1971.

Pollack, Jill S., *Shirley Chisholm,* Franklin Watts, 1994.

Agatha Christie

Born September 15, 1890
Torquay, Devon, England
Died January 12, 1976
Wallingford, England
British author and dramatist
Known as the "Queen of Crime"

"I don't enjoy writing detective stories. I enjoy thinking of a detective story, planning it, but when the time comes to write it, it is like going to work every day, like having a job."

Speaking of her prolific output of novels, stories, and plays, writer Agatha Christie once jokingly claimed, "Oh, I'm an incredible sausage machine." Christie's works have sold well over 400 million copies–a record topped only by the Bible and the plays of sixteenth-century British dramatist William Shakespeare–and have been translated into 103 languages. Her play *The Mousetrap,* originally written as a birthday gift for Queen Mary of England, is the longest-running play in theatrical history. These phenomenal statistics testify to the enduring popularity of Christie's work.

Christie was born Agatha Miller on September 15, 1890, in Torquay, Devon, England, the daughter of Frederick Alvah and Clarissa Boehmer Miller. Tutored at home by her mother until the age of 16, she studied singing and piano in Paris. In 1914 she married Archibald Christie, a colonel in the British Royal Air Corps, with whom she had a daughter, Rosalind. During World War I (1914-1918) she served as a nurse with the Voluntary Aid Detachment in a Red Cross hospital in

Agatha Christie disappears!

Before her divorce from her first husband, Christie herself was the central figure in a mystery that would rival any she created for her novels. On December 3, 1926, her car was found abandoned near Styles, her home in Sunningdale, England. A massive search was immediately organized, involving Christie's family and neighbors and law enforcement officials from four counties. The incident also attracted the attention of the media, fans, and curiosity seekers–over 15,000 of them–and soon vendors had set up stands selling hot drinks and ice cream at the site where Christie's car was discovered. For 10 days the disappearance was the major story in newspapers throughout Britain. Theories of the case offered by "experts" ranged from a vanishing act staged by a brilliant mystery novelist to amnesia and suicide. Christie finally surfaced on December 13 at the Hydropathic Hotel, a fashionable health spa in Harrogate. Although she claimed she had lost her memory as a result of personal problems and had no idea how she had arrived at the hotel, reporters continued to speculate that she had orchestrated a publicity stunt.

Torquay. After divorcing her husband in 1928 Christie traveled extensively. Two years later she married Max Edgar Lucien Mallowen, an archaeologist, and helped him with excavations in Iraq and Syria. During World War II (1939-1945) she worked in the dispensary at University College Hospital in London. Following the war she went with Mallowen to excavate ancient ruins in Assyria, a pattern that was to continue during their happy 46-year marriage as she divided her time between writing and assisting her husband with his archaeological digs. The couple also maintained as many as eight homes at a time, all elegantly furnished and stocked with relics from their travels.

Writes popular mysteries

Christie began writing on a dare from her sister, who challenged her to "write a good detective story." The result was *The Mysterious Affair at Styles,* which was published in 1920. Although the book sold only 2,000 copies and earned

Christie just $70, the publication encouraged her to continue writing. Throughout the 1920s she steadily produced novels, building a loyal following among mystery enthusiasts who liked her clever plots. In 1926 Christie's talent for deceptive plotting came to the attention of the general reading public with *The Murder of Roger Ackroyd.* The ending of the novel–where the murderer is revealed to be a character who is traditionally above suspicion in mystery novels–outraged, surprised, and delighted readers.

Perfects puzzle plot

The Murder of Roger Ackroyd proved to be the first in a long succession of superlative and highly original novels that made Christie's name synonymous with the mystery story. Such books as *Murder on the Orient Express* (1934), *The A.B.C. Murders* (1936), and *Ten Little Indians* (1939) have been acclaimed as the best of Christie's work and, indeed, rank among the finest mystery novels ever written. Over the 50 years of Christie's writing career several factors contributed to the unparalleled popularity of her books. Foremost was her ability to construct a baffling puzzle presented in such a way that the reader's attention is directed away from the most important clues. The solution of the puzzle is always startling but at the same time entirely logical and consistent with the rest of the story. Another feature was Christie's finesse in making even the least suspicious character a possible villain in the crime.

Creates memorable detectives

Perhaps Christie's greatest accomplishment was creating charming and enduring detective characters, the most popular being Hercule Poirot, an eccentric and amusingly self-important Belgian detective. Christie described him as "an extraordinary-looking little man. He was hardly more than five feet, four inches, but carried himself with great dignity. His head was exactly the shape of an egg. His mustache was very still and military. The neatness of his attire was almost incredible. I believe a speck of dust would have caused him more pain than a bullet wound." Poirot's illustrious career came to an end in *Curtain: Hercule Poirot's Last Case* (1975), which was published shortly before Christie's death. Christie had written the book just after World War II and had put it away in a bank vault, intending to have it published after she died. But she decided to enjoy the ending of Poirot's career herself and published the book early. It was hailed as one of Christie's most ingenious stories.

Christie's own favorite among her detectives was Miss Jane Marple, a spinster who lives in St. Mary Mead, a small town in the English countryside. In contrast to Poirot, a professional detective who attributes his success to the use of his "little grey [brain] cells," Miss Marple is an amateur crime solver who depends on intuition and nosiness when solving a crime. She tracks down the criminal on the basis of his or her resemblance to someone she knows in St. Mary Mead, since

Film adaptations of novels and plays by Agatha Christie

Witness for the Prosecution (1957) An unemployed man is accused of murdering a wealthy widow in this adaptation of Christie's story and stage play.

Murder She Said (1962) Miss Marple witnesses a murder on board a train, but the authorities don't seem inclined to believe her.

Murder at the Gallop (1963) Snooping Miss Marple does not believe a rich old man died of natural causes, despite the dissenting police point of view.

Murder on the Orient Express (1974) Hercule Poirot sets out to solve a murder with a trainful of suspects on the elegant *Orient Express* on the trip from Istanbul, Turkey, to Calais, France.

Ten Little Indians (1975) Ten people, gathered on an isolated island under mysterious circumstances, are murdered one by one in an adaptation of Christie's novel and play.

Death on the Nile (1978) Hercule Poirot is called upon to interrupt his vacation to uncover who killed an heiress aboard a steamer cruising down the Nile.

her hometown is the sum total of her knowledge of the world. Some readers have compared Miss Marple to Christie herself, but the author rejected the idea. "I don't have Jane Marple's guilty-till-proven-innocent attitude," she said. "But, like Jane, I don't accept surface appearances."

Becomes successful playwright

While Christie's mystery novels featuring Poirot and Miss Marple enjoyed tremendous success and established her as the most widely read mystery writer of all time, her relatively small output of plays set equally impressive records. Christie is the only playwright to have had three plays running simultaneously in London's theater district, the West End, while another of her plays was being produced off-Broadway in New York City. *The Mousetrap* holds the distinction of being the longest-running play in theatrical history. It has been translated into 22 languages, performed in 41 countries, and seen by millions of people. Despite the success of the work, Christie received no royalties because when the play opened in 1952, she gave the rights to her nine-year-old grandson, who long ago became a millionaire as the result of this gift.

Refines "pure" detective novel

By the time Christie died in 1976 she had made a profound impact upon the writing–and reading–of mystery novels. Although her characters and plots were predictable and her writing style was unremarkable, she has been called the greatest practitioner of the "pure" detective novel. Through the use of plot twists and surprises she was able to keep the reader turning pages until the final word of the story. As one reviewer put it, "There was simply no outguessing Poirot or Miss Marple–or Agatha Christie." During her lifetime Christie received numerous honors and awards, including the Grand Master Award from the Mystery Writers of America and the New York Drama Critics' Circle Award for her play *Witness for the Prosecution.* In 1971 she was named Dame Commander, Order of the British Empire. *The Mousetrap* is still running in London.

Where to learn more

Christie, Agatha, *Agatha Christie: An Autobiography,* Dodd, Mead, 1977.

Morgan, Janet, *Agatha Christie: A Biography,* Alfred A. Knopf, 1985.

Robyns, Gwen, *The Mystery of Agatha Christie,* Doubleday, 1978.

Toye, Randall, *The Agatha Christie Who's Who,* Henry Holt, 1980.

Sandra Cisneros

Born 1954
Chicago, Illinois

Hispanic American writer

The first Chicana to receive a major publishing contract for a work about Chicanas; author of the highly successful book The House on Mango Street

"It was not until this moment when I separated myself, when I considered myself truly distinct, that my writing acquired a voice."

In her poetry and stories, Hispanic American author Sandra Cisneros writes about Mexican and Hispanic American women who find the strength to rise above the poor conditions of their lives. Characters like these women have not been presented so clearly in writing before. Cisneros is determined to introduce them to American readers, and so far her efforts have been successful. A reviewer for the *Washington Post Book World* described Cisneros as "a writer of power and eloquence and great lyrical beauty."

Shyness masks her talent

Cisneros's ability to write about strong characters comes from her childhood experiences. Born in Chicago in 1954, she grew up in poverty. As the only girl in a family of seven children, Cisneros spent most of her time alone. Because her family moved often, she was not able to form lasting friendships. "The moving back and forth, the new school, were very upsetting to me as a child," she once said. "They caused me to be very introverted and shy. I do not remember making friends easily." Instead, Cisneros became a quiet, careful observer of the people and events around her. Writing secretly at home, she recorded feelings she could not express openly.

Because she was too shy to volunteer or speak up in class, Cisneros often received poor grades while attending Catholic schools in Chicago. Yet her Mexican American mother and Mexican father both recognized the importance of education. Her mother made sure all the children had library cards, and her father encouraged them take their studies seriously so they would not have to work as hard for a living as he did. "My father's hands are thick and yellow," Cisneros once wrote in an article for *Glamour,* "stubbed by a history of hammer and nails and twine and coils and springs. 'Use this,' my father said, tapping his head, 'not this,' showing us those hands."

Although Cisneros learned to study hard, she was still too shy to share her creative efforts at school. She felt many of her early teachers were not interested in her experiences. Finally, in the 10th grade, Cisneros was encouraged by one of her teachers to read her work to the class. This teacher also urged her to join the staff of the school's literary magazine, and she eventually became the editor.

Dreams of being a writer

After high school, Cisneros attended Loyola University in Chicago with a major in English. Her father thought she might find a good husband if she went to college, but Cisneros discovered instead a desire to be a writer. After graduating from college she was encouraged by another teacher, who recognized her writing talent, to enroll in the poetry section of the Writer's Workshop at the University of Iowa, a highly respected graduate school for aspiring writers. Cisneros's old fears about sharing her writing with others soon returned. Discovering that many of her classmates had come from more privileged backgrounds, she felt she could not compete with them. As she explained in an interview, "It didn't take me long to learn–after a few days of being there–that nobody cared to hear what I had to say and no one listened to me even when I did speak. I became very frightened and terrified that first year."

Realizes importance of heritage

Cisneros soon realized, however, that although her experiences as a Hispanic American and as a woman were very different, her heritage was just as important as anything her classmates wrote about. "It was not until this moment when I separated myself, when I considered myself truly distinct, that my writing acquired a voice," she later told an interviewer. Out of this insight came her first book, *The House on Mango Street.*

Published in 1984, the book is composed of a series of connected short passages or stories told by Esperanza Cordero, a Hispanic American girl growing up in a Chicago barrio, or Spanish-speaking neighborhood. Much like Cisneros when she was young, Esperanza wants to leave her poor neighborhood to seek a better life for herself. As Esperanza tells her stories, readers come to understand how people live their lives in her neighborhood. Although Esperanza gains enough strength by the end of the book to leave her house on Mango Street, she is reminded by one of the other characters that she must never forget who she is and where she came from: "You will always be Esperanza. You will always be Mango Street. You can't erase what you know. You can't forget who you are."

Moves to California

Since its publication, *The House on Mango Street* has been highly successful. In fact, teachers in junior high schools, high schools, and colleges throughout the country have used the book in their classes. The success of *The House on Mango Street,* however, did not guarantee an easy life for Cisneros. After graduating from the University of Iowa with a master's degree in creative writing, she worked as a part-time teacher. In 1986 she moved to Texas after receiving a fellowship, or a financial award, that would help her finish writing *My Wicked, Wicked Ways,* a book of poetry. After this volume was published in 1987, Cisneros's money ran out. Unemployed but wanting to stay in Texas, she tried to start a private writing program. She even passed out fliers in supermarkets to get people interested in joining, but the program failed. Defeated and broke, Cisneros left Texas to take a teaching job at California State University at Chico.

Signs major publishing contract

While in California, Cisneros received another grant of money, this time from the National Endowment for the Arts, to help her work on a book of fiction. This new award revitalized Cisneros, inspiring her to write *Woman Hollering Creek and Other Stories*. Random House offered to publish the book in 1991, making Cisneros the first Chicana (Mexican American woman) to receive a major publishing contract for a work about Chicanas. A series of short stories about strong Hispanic American women living along the Texas-Mexico border, the collection was praised widely by critics.

Achieves success

In 1994 another large publishing company issued *Loose Woman*, Cisneros's second collection of poetry. A reviewer for

Publishers Weekly, a trade journal in the publishing industry, wrote that the book presents "a powerful, fiercely independent woman of Mexican heritage, though this time the innocence has long been lost." Cisneros says it is important for people of all races in America to understand the lives of Hispanic Americans, especially Hispanic American women. And she feels "honored to give them a form in my writings and to be able to have this material to write about is a blessing."

Where to learn more

Glamour, November 1990, pp. 56-57.

Publishers Weekly, March 29, 1991, pp. 74-75; April 25, 1994, pp. 61-62.

Washington Post Book World, June 9, 1991, p. 3.

Hillary Rodham Clinton

Born October 26, 1947
Park Ridge, Illinois
American first lady
Nationally recognized
attorney; activist on education
and children's issues

H illary Rodham Clinton follows **Eleanor Roosevelt** (see entry) as a first lady who uses her position as a platform for social change. Clinton became the 42nd first lady of the United States on January 20, 1993, when her husband, William (Bill) Clinton, former governor of Arkansas, became president. A nationally known activist on education and children's issues, a mother, and a trusted political adviser to her husband, Hillary Clinton has chaired an Arkansas state commission on education, served on dozens of corporate and civic boards, and made a career as one of America's leading attorneys. She was named one of the nation's top 100 lawyers by the *National Law Review* in 1988 and 1991.

Childhood experience

The eldest of three children of Hugh and Dorothy Rodham, Clinton grew up in the Chicago suburb of Park Ridge, Illinois. Her father owned a fabric store, and her mother was a

"I think that you have to keep true to your own beliefs about what is important, and you have to say it over and over again. But you always have to be open to new ways of saying it that perhaps are understood better."

homemaker who dreamed that her only daughter would one day be the first woman on the U.S. Supreme Court. As a child Clinton was active in ballet, swimming, tennis, skating, softball, and volleyball, and she earned every Brownie and Girl Scout badge.

Clinton's advocacy for children's rights grew out of her religious upbringing. Having learned fairness from her parents, she learned about social justice from her youth minister, Reverend Don Jones. Her church group looked after migrant children while their parents worked and also visited inner-city Chicago residents. Clinton staged sporting events and a small circus to raise funds for poor urban children as an expession of social responsibility.

College speech

In high school Clinton was class president, a member of the student council, the debating team, the National Honor Society, and the winner of Maine South High School's first social science award. After graduation, she attended Wellesley College in Wellesley, Massachusetts, at a time when college students were protesting the Vietnam War. The assassination of clergyman and civil rights leader Martin Luther King, Jr., deeply affected Clinton. She had met King when Rev. Jones had taken her to hear him preach in 1962. Clinton graduated from Wellesley with honors and became the first student at the college to speak at commencement. As president of the student government, she had polled her classmates on what she should say, soliciting their poems and ideas and communicating the turmoil of a country facing an unpopular war, political assassinations, and rioting in cities. The speech brought the audience to its feet as they applauded the new graduate. The event was featured in *Life* magazine, giving Clinton her first national media exposure.

Meets Bill Clinton

Clinton next attended Yale Law School in New Haven, Connecticut, where she wrote her now-famous thesis on the rights of children and worked with poor youths at the Yale-New Haven Hospital. She also met two of the most influential people in her life: Bill Clinton and **Marian Wright Edelman** (see entry). Edelman was the founder of the Children's Defense Fund (CDF), a Washington-based lobbying group. Clinton first noticed Bill Clinton when he was trying to convince a group of classmates that they did not need immunization shots to visit Arkansas and boasting that Arkansas had "the biggest watermelons in the world." She met him again while registering for classes, and they talked for an hour. When they reached the front of the line, the registrar said, "Bill, what are you doing here? You already registered."

After graduation in 1973, Bill Clinton and Hillary Rodham went their separate ways. He returned to Arkansas to teach and run for Congress (he lost), and she went to Cambridge, Massachusetts, to work for the CDF as a staff lawyer and board chairperson. Then she went to Washington, D.C., to work on the impeachment inquiry of President Richard Nixon, who was in trouble because of his apparent involvment in the Watergate cover-up. The gravest scandal in American history, the break-in at the Watergate hotel and the attempted cover-up, seemed to have been sanctioned by the president in an effort to win him re-election in 1972. In 1974 Hillary Rodham took a teaching job at the University of Arkansas Law School, then married Bill Clinton in 1975. Using her maiden name, Rodham, she continued to teach and headed the legal aid clinic at the school. In 1977 she joined the Rose Law Firm in Little Rock, Arkansas, and within two years became the firm's first woman partner.

Faces surname controversy

In 1978 Bill Clinton was elected governor of Arkansas, but he lost his bid for re-election two years later. Reports surfaced of voter resentment that Hillary had never adopted her husband's surname and that Bill Clinton brought outsiders into state government. Two years later, when Clinton was re-elected, Hillary Rodham began using Clinton as her surname. She chaired the Arkansas Education Standards Committee, an unpaid public position; she traveled the state, held meetings, visited schools, and testified before state legislators; and she oversaw a committee study that led to new standards for public schools, including teacher testing and smaller class sizes.

Throughout her husband's 12 years as governor, Clinton continually helped children's causes. She initiated the Home Instruction Program for Preschool Youth and sat on the board of the state's Children's Hospital, where she helped establish Arkansas's first neonatal nursery. She also served on the Southern Governors' Association Task Force on Infant Mortality. In 1982 Hillary Clinton gave birth to a daughter, Chelsea. Determined that Chelsea would have as normal an upbringing as possible, the Clintons have kept their daughter out of the media spotlight.

Supports husband's presidential ambitions

At the onset of the 1992 presidential campaign, many Democratic presidential hopefuls believed President George Bush was unbeatable because of his popularity after the Gulf War. Thinking otherwise, the Clintons mutually decided that Bill Clinton could become the next president. However, the campaign almost immediately turned stormy as critics tried to discredit both Clintons. After charges of infidelity surfaced against Bill Clinton, Hillary defended her marriage on the television program "60 Minutes." Her outspokenness sometimes made her a campaign issue.

She was often quoted as saying, "If you vote for him, you get me." When asked by the press if her career as a lawyer conflicted with the responsibilities of a first lady, Clinton replied, "I suppose I could have stayed home and baked cookies and had teas, but what I decided to do is fulfill my profession. The work that I have done as a professional, a public advocate, has been aimed ... to assure that women can make the choices ... whether it's a full-time career, full-time motherhood, or some combination." The media zeroed in on the "cookie" comment, fueling a new controversy.

The campaign also focused attention on Clinton's legal writings, some of them 20 years old and dating from law school. She had once written that the rights of children are often ignored by courts and that at one time in history women, like slaves, had no rights. As a result her critics accused her of encouraging children to sue their parents over trivial matters and equating marriage with slavery.

Heads task force

Soon after President Clinton's inauguration, people wondered what responsibility he would give his wife, and many feared she would have too much political power and influence. The president announced that Hillary Rodham Clinton would take the unpaid position of chair of a task force charged with producing a health care reform plan. No first lady had ever been

First Ladies

First lady is the formal title of the wife of the president of the United States. Although the position pays no salary, the first lady has an office, a staff, and many official duties that have evolved since Martha Washington, the wife of the first president, lived in the White House. A major responsibility of the first lady is being a host with the president at formal state dinners and other ceremonial occasions requiring dignity and solemnity. Each first lady is noted for a particular concern. For instance, Jacqueline Kennedy redecorated the White House and showed the nation the interior changes in a television interview. Ladybird Johnson took on the project of beautifying America's landscape. Betty Ford founded the Betty Ford Clinic to treat drug addiction and alcoholism. Many first ladies have been close political advisers to their husbands. Rosalyn Carter attended presidential cabinet meetings. Nancy Reagan also had an influence on her husband's political thinking.

given such an important assignment. The goal of the task force was to produce a health care system that would insure all Americans, but the plan was not accepted by Congress.

In the spring of 1995 Clinton, accompanied by her daughter, completed a 12-day goodwill tour of southern Asia during which they met with heads of state and ordinary citizens. Clinton observed such things as health care procedures and banking practices. Clinton renewed her commitment to women's issues on this trip and worked toward a declaration of principles on the rights of women at the annual United Nations conference on women held in Beijing, China, in September 1995. Clinton is the honorary chairperson of the American delegation.

Where to learn more

Guernsey, JoAnn Bren, *Hillary Rodham Clinton: A New Kind of First Lady,* Lerner Publications, 1993.

Levert, Susanne, *Hillary Rodham Clinton,* Millbrook Press, 1994.

Radcliffe, Donnie, *Hillary Rodham Clinton: A First Lady for Our Time,* Warner Books, 1993.

Sherrow, Victoria, *Hillary Rodham Clinton,* Dillon Press, 1993.

Stacey, T. J., *Hillary Rodham Clinton: Activist First Lady,* Enslow Publishers, 1994.

Jewel Plummer Cobb

Born January 17, 1924
Chicago, Illinois

African American cell biologist,
educator, and administrator

Conducts research into the action
and interaction of living cells

Jewel Plummer Cobb is known for her contributions to the field of cell biology and for promoting minority involvement in the sciences. She has focused much of her research on melanin, a brown or black skin pigment, and the causes and growth of normal and cancerous pigment cells. Her research into the effects of drugs on cancer cells was important to future research in the field of chemotherapy (the use of chemicals in treating disease). As an educator Cobb initiated a number of programs to encourage participation of ethnic minorities and women in the sciences.

Born in Chicago January 17, 1924, Cobb was the only child of Frank and Carriebel (Cole) Plummer. Her father was a physician and a graduate of Cornell University in Ithaca, New York. Her mother taught dance in public schools and also participated in the Works Projects Administration, a government-sponsored jobs program during the Great Depression, a period of worldwide economic crisis during the 1930s.

"When I see more black students in the laboratories than I see on the football field, then I'll be happy."

Cobb's paternal grandfather was a pharmacist who graduated from Howard University in Washington, D.C.

Family values education

Cobb's upper-middle-class background introduced her to many black professionals and their children while she grew up, and she spent summer vacations at a northern Michigan resort. Although the public schools in Chicago were largely segregated, Cobb received a solid education that was enriched by exposure to her father's library at home. Her interest in biology was sparked in her sophomore year by her first look through the lens of a microscope.

After graduation the high school honor society student attended the University of Michigan, where housing was segregated. After three semesters Cobb transferred to Talladega College in Talladega, Alabama, and earned a degree in biology in 1944. She then accepted a teaching fellowship at New York University in New York City, although she was at first turned down for admission. Her poise and credentials finally tipped the scales in her favor, however, and she maintained a graduate fellowship for five years in cell physiology.

Pursues career as cell biologist

By 1950 Cobb had completed a master's degree and a doctorate. Because she enjoyed research and a theoretical approach to biology, she decided to become a cell biologist. Focusing on the action and interaction of living cells, she was particularly interested in tissue culture, in which cells are grown outside of the body and studied under microscopes. She also studied how new cancer-fighting drugs affected cancer cells. Cobb has held a series of research positions at various colleges and research facilities throughout the United States. She was a fellow at the National Cancer Institute for two years after receiving her doctorate, and from 1952 to 1954 she was the director of the Tissue Culture Laboratory at the University of Illinois. At the end of this period Cobb married, and in 1957 she and her husband had a son. In 1960

Cobb was appointed professor of biology at Sarah Lawrence College in Bronxville, New York, where she taught and continued her research into skin pigment. She was particularly interested in melanoma, or skin cancer, and the ability of the pigment melanin to protect skin from damage caused by ultraviolet light.

Establishes minority programs

In 1969, two years after she and her husband divorced, Cobb was appointed dean and professor of zoology at Connecticut College in New London, Connecticut. In addition to teaching and continuing her research, she established a privately funded premedical graduate program and a predental program for minority students. Although used by numerous other colleges as models, these programs were discontinued after Cobb left Connecticut in 1976. For the next five years she served as dean and professor of biological sciences at Douglass College. While Cobb gave up her research in order to fulfill her administrative and teaching obligations, she continued to press for the advancement of minorities and women in the sciences. She wrote about the difficulties women face in scientific fields in a 1979 paper, "Filters for Women in Science." Cobb argues that various pressures, particularly in the educational system, act as filters that prevent many women from choosing science careers. The socialization of girls, she says, discourages them from pursuing mathematics and science from a very early age. She further noted that even women who moved past such obstacles have struggled to get university tenure and the same jobs (at equal pay) as men.

Becomes university president

In 1981 Cobb was named president of California State University (CSU) at Fullerton. She initiated the construction of engineering and science buildings and established a program for ethnic students. Extending her work to the community, she founded a privately funded center for the study of aging. Cobb became a trustee professor at California State College in Los

Angeles in 1990, and the following year she was made principal investigator for Southern California Science and Engineering ACCESS Center and Network. A trustee of several colleges and recipient of numerous honorary degrees, Cobb worked with a consortium of six colleges to raise private funds for grants and fellowships for minorities in science and engineering. Over the years Cobb had become increasingly aware of the disparity between the number of black men in sports and those in the lab. As part of the consortium effort, faculty members tutored students on an individual basis in order to solidify their math skills, which Cobb felt were a crucial foundation for a career in the sciences. President emeritus of CSU since 1990, Cobb continues to use her skill as an educator, administrator, and scientist to promote education and careers for minorities in the sciences.

Where to learn more

Cobb, Jewel Plummer, "Filters for Women in Science," in *Expanding the Role of Women in the Sciences,* edited by Anne M. Briscoe and Sheila M. Pfafflin, New York Academy of Sciences, 1979, pp. 236-48.

Cobb, Jewel Plummer, "The Role of Women Presidents/Chancellors in Intercollegiate Athletics," in *Women at the Helm,* edited by J. A. Sturnick, J. E. Milley, and C. A. Tisinger, AASCU Press, 1991, pp. 42-50.

Hine, Darlene Clark, editor, *Black Women in America: An Historical Encyclopedia,* Carlson Publishing, 1993, pp. 257-58.

Jacqueline Cochran

Born 1910(?)
Pensacola, Florida

Died August 9, 1980
Indio, California

American aviatrix;
business entrepreneur

Holder of many world
aviation speed records

Jacqueline Cochran rose from extreme poverty to become an aviatrix who held more speed, distance, and altitude records than any other living pilot. She was awarded the Distinguished Service Medal for her involvement during World War II (1939-1945) in organizing the Women's Airforce Service Pilots, called WASPs. Besides setting world aviation speed records, Cochran was a successful businesswoman who developed a line of cosmetics sold nationally and with her husband operated a ranch in California.

"With my last breath, I'll be on the aerial sidelines cheering those who are carrying on."

Nearly always hungry

Cochran was born in Pensacola, Florida, around 1910 (her birth date is unknown) and orphaned when she was a baby. She grew up in the worst possible conditions in sawmill camp towns. She had no shoes, wore dresses made from old flour sacks, and was nearly always hungry except when she could get food for herself by catching crabs or fish. When she found out her assumed parents were really foster parents, she broke away from them. She soon met a Catholic priest and a teacher who clothed and cared for her. At age eight Cochran worked in the cotton mills of Columbus, Georgia, at six cents an hour. Putting in long hours under bad conditions, she was able to buy her first pair of shoes. She then took a job at a beauty parlor and learned how to give permanent waves. Her next job was in Montgomery, Alabama, in a department store beauty parlor. After a customer recommended a nursing program at a local hospital, Cochran enrolled and graduated in three years. Moving again to Pensacola to work in a beauty parlor, Cochran attended dances at the local naval flying school.

Learns to fly

Cochran decided to move north, working at the Saks Fifth Avenue beauty salon in a job that kept her six months in New York City and six months in Miami, Florida. During this time she started a cosmetics business and met a number of wealthy people. One was Floyd Bostwick Odlum, whom she would eventually marry in 1936. An aircraft manufacturer, Odlum was instrumental in Cochran's decision to learn how to fly. Using her vacation time, she began take flying lessons at Roosevelt Field on Long Island (New York) in 1932. Within three days she was flying solo (even though she did not know how to read a compass) and within three weeks she was a licensed pilot. Cochran moved to San Diego, California, to enter flying school, but she was soon disillusioned by the lack of flying time. Finally, a friend who was an air officer on the battleship *West Virginia* agreed to teach her. She bought an old airplane and he instructed her according to the navy method, although she earned a commercial pilot's license.

Joins war effort

Cochran entered her first Bendix transcontinental air race in 1935. Placing third in the 1937 race, she won first place the next year and received praise from the public and male competitors. When World War II broke out in Europe, Cochran knew female pilots would be needed. She began by flying a bomber to England in June 1941. Rising to the rank of flight

captain in the British Air Transport Auxiliary, Cochran trained women to fly new aircraft throughout Europe from manufacturer to military site. In 1942 the U.S. Army air forces chose her to head its woman pilot training program. The following year she was appointed head of the Women's Airforce Service Pilots (WASPs), a unit that flew transport planes. After organizing the WASPs Cochran became a correspondent with *Liberty* magazine in the Pacific Theater (in the South Pacific), reporting on

Jet aviation records

After World War II the next generation of jet-propelled aircraft was introduced, and Cochran played a major role in testing the planes. In 1953 she was the first woman to fly faster than the speed of sound (breaking the sound barrier). She also set a number of speed records for both men and women, flying a Sabrejet (a military aircraft). Among her records were 100 kilometers, or 652.552 miles per hour; 500 kilometers, or 590.321 miles per hour; and 15 kilometers, or 675.471 miles per hour. Eight years later Cochran broke the 100 kilometer and 500 kilometer records, this time flying a Northrop T-38. She also set a new altitude record of 55,253 feet. Cochran continued to set records in the 1960s. Flying an A3J, she became the first woman to reach Mach 2 (twice the speed of sound). Cochran was the first woman to land a jet on an aircraft carrier, the USS *Independence*. She was also the first woman to fly a jet aircraft across the Atlantic Ocean, traveling 5,120 miles from New Orleans, Louisiana, to Hanover, West Germany, on April 7, 1962. Piloting a Lockheed F-104G Starfighter jet, Cochran flew 1,273.10 miles an hour in a 15-25 kilometer straightaway course and 1,203.94 miles an hour in a 100 kilometer closed course.

the Japanese surrender. Although Cochran was unable to devote time to her cosmetics business during the war years, it nonetheless prospered with millions of dollars worth of products being sold.

Wins awards

Cochran won numerous honors for her flying exploits, beginning with the Billy Mitchell Trophy in 1938. She served two terms as the first woman president of Federation Aeronautique Inernationale. Honorary wings were awarded to her by the French, Chinese, Turkish, Spanish, and Royal Thailand air forces. Knowing from her own background the hardship caused by poor educational opportunities, Cochran volunteered on the national board of directors of the Camp Fire Girls for nine years. In 1954 Cochran wrote her autobiography, *The Stars at Noon,* in which she told her story of triumphing over poverty to reach the highest achievements. After her retirement from the U.S. Air Force Reserve in 1970, Cochran served as a consultant to the National Aeronautics and Space Administration. Cochran died on August 9, 1980, in Indio, California.

Where to learn more

Cochran, Jacqueline, *The Stars at Noon,* Little, 1954.

Cochran, Jacqueline (with Maryann Brinley Bucknum), *Jackie Cochran: An Autobiography,* Bantam Books, 1987.

Fisher, Marquita O., *Jacqueline Coch-ran: First Lady of Flight,* Garrard, 1973.

Smith, Elizabeth Simpson, *Coming Out Right: The Story of Jacqueline Cochran,* Walker and Co., 1991.

Bessie Coleman

Born January 26, 1893
Atlanta, Texas
Died April 30, 1926
African American aviator
First black woman to receive
a pilot's license; popular stunt pilot

"If I can create the minimum of my plans and desires, there shall be no regrets."

During the early 1920s, a young African American manager of a chili restaurant in Chicago decided she wanted more out of life. The newspapers were filled with stories of the latest exploits of a new group of adventurers known as aviators. Deciding to be an aviator, too, Bessie Coleman pursued her dream across the ocean and became the first African American woman to receive a pilot's license. She soon became a popular stunt and exhibition flier, thrilling thousands with her daring stunts. Although she died in an accident when she was only 33, Coleman inspired an entire generation of African American aviators.

Manages chili restaurant in Chicago

Coleman was born in Atlanta, Texas, and her family moved to Waxahachie, near Dallas, Texas, while she was still a young girl. Her father was three-quarters American Indian, and he returned to Indian Territory when Coleman was seven years old. Her mother, Susan Coleman, supported the family–four daughters and a son–by picking cotton and doing laundry. The children also worked whenever they could. Although Susan Coleman could not read or write at that time, she encouraged her children to get an education.

After finishing high school, Bessie Coleman wanted to go to college. Her mother let her keep the money she made from washing and ironing to pay her college expenses. She enrolled at Langston Industrial College (now Langston University) in Oklahoma, but college cost more than she expected. Coleman dropped out after one semester, moved to Chicago, and took a manicuring course. Coleman eventually found work at the White Sox Barber Shop on 35th Street near State Street. Later she managed a chili restaurant on the same street.

Becomes interested in aviation

Coleman had always been interested in reading, and she used her spare moments reading about current affairs. She also became interested in the new field of aviation. Looking for a new challenge, she decided to learn how to fly and get her pilot's license. Coleman was soon discouraged when all of her applications for entering aviation schools were rejected. A close friend, Robert S. Abbott, founder and editor of the *Chicago Defender* newspaper, encouraged her to learn French and study aviation overseas. She took his advice, went to Europe, and took lessons from French and German pilots. Coleman also studied under the chief aviator for Anthony Fokker's aircraft corporation and learned to fly the highly regarded German Fokker airplane.

Receives her pilot's license

Coleman returned briefly to the United States in 1921 with her pilot's license. She made another trip to Europe, then headed back to the United States in 1922 with her international pilot's license. It was a remarkable feat: Coleman was the first African American woman to earn pilot's licenses only 10 years after the first American woman ever to be licensed and less than 20 years after aviators Orville and Wilbur Wright made their historic flight in 1903. Barnstorming, or stunt flying, was a popular

Coleman takes a stand

Coleman was once offered a role in a featurelength film titled *Shadow and Sunshine,* to be financed by the African American Seminole Film Producing Company. She gladly accepted, hoping the publicity would help to advance her career and provide her with some of the money she needed to establish her own flying school. But upon learning that the first scene in the movie required her to appear in tattered clothes, with a walking stick and a pack on her back, she refused to proceed. Although Coleman's stand alienated her from some of the most powerful men in the black entertainment world, she did not want to add to the negative image that many whites had of most blacks.

attraction in the United States and the main area of aviation open to women, so Coleman decided to become a stunt and exhibition flier.

During the Labor Day weekend in 1922, Coleman made her first appearance in an air show at Curtiss Field near New York City, sponsored by her friend Abbott and the *Chicago Defender.* Coleman repeated her performance six weeks later at the Checker board Airdrome (now Midway Airport) in Chicago, again sponsored by Abbott. Her manager was David L. Behncke, founder and president of the International Airline Pilots Association.

Coleman soon became known as "Brave Bessie" for her aviation exploits. She participated in air shows across the country, including her hometown of Waxahachie. She gave lectures on the opportunities in aviation at schools and churches wherever she went. While in California, she did some aerial advertising for the Firestone Rubber Company.

One of Coleman's lifelong dreams was to establish her own aviation school, where young African Americans could learn to fly and prepare for aviation careers. She saved money from her barnstorming and lecturing jobs, and by early 1926 she wrote to her sister Elois that she was on the verge of reaching her dream.

Tragedy at the air show

At the end of April 1926, Coleman accepted an invitation from the Negro Welfare League to perform in a Memorial Day air show. On April 30, 1926, Coleman and her mechanic, William D. Wills, made a practice run with the mechanic piloting the plane. During one of the maneuvers the plane's controls jammed. Coleman, who was not wearing a seat belt, was catapulted out of the plane and fell to her death. Wills tried but failed to regain control of the aircraft, and died instantly when it hit the ground. Although the wreckage of the plane was badly burned, it was later discovered that a wrench used to service the engine had slid into the gearbox and jammed it, causing the plane to spin out of control. Just before the accident, she had chanced to meet her longtime supporter Robert Abbott in a restaurant in Jacksonville, Florida, and they had had a reunion.

A few years later Bessie Coleman Aero Clubs were active, with many African American fliers in the membership. A monthly publication, the *Bessie Coleman Aero News,* was circulated to these clubs in May 1930, with William J. Powell as editor. Powell also wrote *Black Wings,* a book about African American aviators, in 1934. The front of the book features a picture of Coleman in her flying uniform. Powell dedicated the book to "the memory of Bessie Coleman ... who ... displayed courage equal to that of the most daring men."

Honored for achievements

African American aviators have paid tribute to Coleman by flying in formation over Lincoln Cemetery on Memorial Day and dropping flowers on her grave. In 1975 the Bessie Coleman Aviators Organization was formed in the Chicago area by young black women actively interested in aviation and aerospace. In 1990 a 51-foot-long mural was unveiled at Lambert-Saint Louis International Airport commemorating black achievements in aviation from 1917 to 1990. Titled *Black Americans in Flight* and painted by Spencer Taylor, it depicts 75 men and women pioneers in aviation, including Coleman.

Where to learn more

Goodrich, James, "Salute to Bessie Coleman," *Negro Digest,* No. 8 (May 1950), pp. 82-83.

King, Anita, "Brave Bessie: First Black Pilot," *Essence* No. 7 (May 1976), p. 36; No. 7 (June 1976), p. 48.

Powell, William J., *Black Wings,* Ivan Deach, Jr., 1934.

Rich, Doris L., *Queen Bess: Daredevil Aviator,* Smithsonian Institution Press, 1993.

St. Laurent, Philip, "Bessie Coleman, Aviator," *Tuesday,* January 9, 1973, pp. 10, 12.

Gerty T. Cori

Born August 15, 1896
Prague, Czechoslovakia

Died October 26, 1957

Austro-Hungarian-born American
biochemist

Won the Nobel Prize in
physiology/medicine in 1947
for research on sugar metabolism

"I believe that in art and science are the glories of the human mind. I see no conflict between them."

Gerty T. Cori made significant contributions in two major areas of biochemistry that increased understanding of how the body stores and uses sugars and other carbohydrates. During her early scientific career, Cori performed pioneering research on sugar metabolism (how sugars supply energy to the body) in collaboration with her husband, Carl Ferdinand Cori. For their work they shared the 1947 Nobel Prize in physiology/medicine with Bernardo A. Houssay, who had conducted studies in the same field. Cori later focused on diseases called glycogen storage disorders, demonstrating that these illnesses are caused by disruptions in sugar metabolism. Both phases of her work showed other scientists the importance of studying enzymes in order to understand normal metabolism and disease processes.

Cori was born in the city of Prague, then part of the Austro-Hungarian Empire, on August 15, 1896. She was the first of three daughters of Otto and Martha Neustadt Radnitz. Cori's family background influenced her later choice of a career. Her father was a manager of sugar refineries and her maternal uncle, a professor of pediatrics (medical care of children), encouraged her to pursue her interests in science. After being tutored at home, Cori enrolled in a private girls school. At that time girls were not expected to pursue advanced education, so in order to follow her dream of becoming a chemist, she first studied at the Tetschen Realgymnasium.

In 1914 Cori entered medical school at the German University of Prague (Ferdinand University) where she met Carl Ferdinand Cori, a classmate who shared her interest in scientific research. Together they studied human complement, the first of a lifelong series of collaborations. In 1920, after receiving their doctor of medicine degrees, they moved to Vienna and were married. Carl worked at the University of Vienna and the University of Graz, while Gerty took a position as an assistant at the Karolinen Children's Hospital. Noticing that some of her young patients suffered from a disease called congenital myxedema, she became interested in how the thyroid gland influences body temperature regulation.

Immigrates to United States

After World War I (1914-1918), Europe was in the midst of great social and economic unrest. Because food was scarce, Cori suffered briefly from malnourishment while working in Vienna. Under these conditions the Coris future in scientific careers seemed bleak. In 1922 Carl Cori took a position as a biochemist at New York State Institute for the Study of Malignant Diseases (later the Roswell Park Memorial Institute) in Buffalo, New York. Cori joined him a few months later as an assistant pathologist at the same institution.

Gerty Cori with her
husband, Carl, in their
laboratory at Washington
University in 1947.

Collaborates with husband

Colleagues cautioned the Coris against working together, arguing that collaboration would hurt Carl's career. However, Gerty's duties as an assistant pathologist allowed her some free time, which she used to begin a study of carbohydrate metabolism with her husband. During their years in Buffalo, they jointly published a number of papers on sugar metabolism that influenced the thinking of other scientists. In 1928 the Coris became naturalized citizens of the United States. Three years later they moved to St. Louis, Missouri, where Gerty took a position as research associate at Washington University School of Medicine and Carl was a professor. The Coris' son, Carl Thomas, was born in 1936.

Receives Nobel Prize

Cori became a research associate professor of biochemistry in 1943, then, in 1947, a full professor of biochemistry. During the 1930s and 1940s, as the Coris continued their research on sugar metabolism, their laboratory gained an international reputation as an important center of biochemical breakthroughs. For their pivotal studies in sugar metabolism, the Coris were awarded the Nobel Prize for physiology or medicine in 1947, an honor they shared with Argentine physiologist Bernardo A. Houssay. Gerty Cori was just the third woman to receive a Nobel Prize in science, after **Marie Curie** and **Irène Joloit-Curie** (see entries). Like the previous women winners, Cori was a corecipient of the prize with her husband.

Conducts significant research

In the 1920s, when the Coris began to study carbohydrate metabolism, it was generally believed that the sugar called glucose, a type of carbohydrate, was formed from another carbohydrate, glycogen, by the addition of water molecules in a process known as hydrolysis. However, in the course of their work they discovered a chemical compound, glucose-1-phosphate, made up of glucose and a phosphate group that is derived from glycogen by the action of an enzyme called phosphorylase. Their finding was the basis for the later understanding of sugar metabolism and carbohydrates.

Studies insulin

Cori had been interested in hormones since her early thyroid research in Vienna. The discovery of the hormone insulin in 1921 stimulated her to examine its role in sugar metabolism. The capacity of insulin to control diabetes gave great importance to these investigations. After extensive study and experimentation the Coris found that glycogen is converted to glucose by an enzyme called phosphoglucomutase, which gave them a fairly complete picture of carbohydrate metabolism. Their discovery changed the way scientists thought about reactions in the human body.

Returns to pediatric medicine

In her later years Cori turned her attention to a group of inherited childhood diseases known collectively as glycogen storage disorders. She determined the structure of the highly branched glycogen molecule in 1952. She found that diseases of glycogen storage fall into two general groups, one involving too much glycogen and the other showing abnormal glycogen. Cori thus opened new fields of study to other scientists. Later she was instrumental in the discovery of a number of other chemical compounds and enzymes that play key roles in biological processes. At the time of her death, on October 26, 1957, Cori's influence on the field of biochemistry was enormous. In recognition of her accomplishments she was awarded the prestigious Garvan Medal for women chemists from the American Chemical Society as well as membership in the National Academy of Sciences.

Where to learn more

Magill, F. N., editor, *The Nobel Prize Winners, Physiology or Medicine,* Volume 2: *1944-1969,* Salem Press, 1991, pp. 550-59.

Veglahn, Nancy J., *Women Scientists,* Facts on File, 1991, pp. 57-63.

Mairead Corrigan

Born January 27, 1944
Belfast, Northern Ireland

Betty Williams

Born May 22, 1943
Belfast, Northern Ireland

Irish peace activists
Corecipients of the 1976
Nobel Peace Prize

L iving in a Northern Ireland racked by a conflict between the Catholic Irish Republican Army (IRA) and factions loyal to Britain, Mairead Corrigan and Betty Williams were brought together as a result of one of the region's numerous acts of violence. One witnessed the tragedy, the other was related to the victims. Both agreed that the killing of armed combatants and innocent women and children must cease, so they joined forces in an attempt to bring an end to the violence. Their efforts, which were credited with reducing the death toll in Northern Ireland by half, earned the two women a Nobel Peace Prize.

Lifelong commitment to community

Corrigan was the second child in a family of five girls and two boys. She attended Catholic schools but was forced to leave at the age of 14 because her family was not able to pay the tuition. At this time Corrigan's desire to help people in the

"We want for our children, as we want for ourselves, our lives at home, at work, and at play to be lives of joy and peace." (Declaration of the Peace People)

The separation of Ireland

The British took control of Ireland in the late thirteenth century. The Irish resisted British rule with frequent but unsuccessful rebellions until 1922, when the Irish Free State was established. At that time the country was divided into the predominantly Catholic, 26-county Republic of Ireland in the south and six counties with a Protestant majority and a Catholic minority, called Northern Ireland, that remained part of the United Kingdom. Since many people in Northern Ireland, such as the IRA, refused to recognize this division, a campaign for a united Ireland began. In the late 1960s the British government sent in military troops to act as a "police force." This action served only to escalate the conflict between the IRA and groups loyal to Britain—the Ulster Defense League, the Ulster Volunteer Force, the Ulster Freedom Fighters, and the Red Hand Commandos—during which more than 3,000 people were killed.

community became apparent when she joined the Legion of Mary, a Catholic lay (not part of the clergy) organization. In her youth Corrigan was influenced by the traditions of Catholicism, but not by the traditions of the Republicans, those factions of Northern Ireland's Catholic minority who sought to unite the province with the Republic of Ireland.

Williams was born on May 22, 1943, in Belfast, Northern Ireland, into a family of mixed religions. Her Jewish grandfather, Catholic mother, and Protestant father taught her to turn away from bigotry. When Williams was 13 her mother was left incapacitated by a stroke and she took on the role of raising her younger sister. After attending Catholic schools and later a trade school she worked as a secretary. Then she was drawn into the public arena by an event common on the streets of Belfast: On August 10, 1976, Anne Maguire and her three children were out for a walk when they were hit by a runaway IRA car. All three children were killed.

Community for Peace People

Maguire was Corrigan's sister. After the tragedy Corrigan appeared on television with her brother-in-law, Jackie Maguire, to condemn the violence of the IRA. In a separate action, Williams, who witnessed the killing of the children, immediately circulated a petition. Going from door to door, she soon collected 6,000 signatures, then appeared on television two days after the deaths to present the petition. At the funeral for the Maguire children Corrigan and Williams joined forces and agreed to work for peace. They founded an organization that they first called Women for Peace but later renamed Commu-

nity for Peace People. By the end of the first month 30,000 women were demonstrating for peace, and by the third march Catholics and Protestants had become allies instead of enemies. The marchers, especially Corrigan and Williams, were suspected by both sides of "collaborating with the enemy." At times they were severely beaten and their lives were threatened. Yet they persisted, spreading the word of their movement throughout the world.

Betty Williams (left) and Mairead Corrigan (right) display some of the hundreds of telegrams of support they received from all over the world.

Reeducation and action the key

Corrigan was convinced that the killing would stop only after considerable reeducation. "I think one of the things the peace movement has to do," she said, "is to persuade the members of the different paramilitary organizations that there is a way other than with pistols and rifles. After all, those things have been tried and obviously have not worked." She believes conventional education and attitudes perpetuate the old hatreds

In September 1994 the IRA called a cease fire in Northern Ireland. The following month the Ulster Volunteer Force, the Ulster Freedom Fighters, and the Red Hand Commandos also declared a halt to hostilities, but the Ulster Defense League did not join in the resolution. These actions led to peace talks involving the governments of Northern Ireland, the Republic of Ireland, and Great Britain. After considerable debate Sinn Fein, the political wing of the IRA, was also included in the discussions. While negotiations continued there were no killings and British troops began to leave Northern Ireland.

because people are not taught to question. "Unfortunately, we never question our educational system," she said. "If we stop to evaluate a lot of our old ideas and concepts, we find that they're myths, that they're false; and that bigotry has created the fear and the hatred that divides our people."

Finding no sense in the violence, Williams turned to the peace movement to give voice to her views. "We reached a point, I think, when we can no longer remain passive, when we feel that we must do something," she said. "What changed my outlook was ... that I actually saw a young soldier killed before my eyes in the city. At that moment I asked myself: Are you going to keep on doing nothing, or are you going to do something?" The goal of her activism became the unification of all of Northern Ireland. To IRA calls for peace with justice, she responded: "Where was the justice in the death of a child not yet three years old? ... All I could see was that young men and boys of my area were becoming violent, aggressive, almost murderers; and that they were rapidly becoming the heroes of the community. Was that justice?" The organization founded by Williams and Corrigan was vital to the future of Northern Ireland. Williams said "What we're doing is absolutely necessary to save lives.... [The Peace People] are a very serious organization that is going to change the structures of the province."

Nobel Peace Prize

For their work, Corrigan and Williams received worldwide recognition. In 1976 they were awarded the Carl von Ossietzky Prize of the Federal Republic of Germany. The following year they were given honorary degrees by Yale University in New Haven, Connecticut, and in Oslo, Norway, they accepted donations of $340,000 to be used for expansion of the Peace People. In October 1977 they were awarded the Nobel Peace Prize. Corrigan and Williams announced their resignations from the Peace People in April 1978. Williams eventually left Belfast for the United States, while Corrigan later returned to the Peace People. With the membership of the organization declining, Corrigan continued her efforts to reconcile the two warring factions in Northern Ireland.

Where to learn more

Conta, Marcia Maher, *Women for Human Rights,* Raintree, 1979.

Deutsch, Richard, *Mairead Corrigan/Betty Williams,* Woodbury, 1977.

Edith Cresson

Born January 27, 1934
Boulogne-sur-Seine, France

French politician

First woman ever appointed
prime minister of France

"The U.S. is a great democracy. Japan is not. We have the same culture. Do we want Europe to become a Japanese colony?"

When Edith Cresson was appointed prime minister of France on May 15, 1991, she became the first woman in the history of France to hold the position. President Francois Mitterand's political reasons for appointing Cresson had more to do with salvaging his weakened Socialist party than with making history. In elevating Cresson, Mitterand turned to an old friend and political ally to replace a prime minister, Michel Rocard, who did not share his social goals. Cresson brought to the position years of experience in Socialist politics, French government, and international economic affairs. In her short time as prime minister she drew intense attention and controversy for her outspoken attacks on Japanese business. At the same time she battled French prejudice against women in politics, an issue she had to deal with throughout her career.

Advanced education precedes her political life

Cresson was born Edith Campion on January 27, 1934, in Boulogne-sur-Seine, France, the daughter of Gabriel Campion, a civil servant, and his wife Jacqueline (Vignal) Campion. She received an undergraduate degree in business at the Haute Etudes Commerciales (School of Higher Commercial Studies) and later a Ph.D. in demography, or the study of human populations. In 1959 she married Jacques Cresson, a business executive. She became active in French politics in 1965 when she joined the Convention of Republican Institutions, the forerunner of the current Socialist party. She supported Mitterand during his unsuccessful presidential campaign in 1966, and the two have remained close friends since. Cresson joined his newly formed Socialist party in 1971 and spent several years functioning as the party's secretary, responsible for organizing youth and student chapters.

Nicknamed "The Fighter"

Cresson revealed her forthrightness and tenacity early in her political career. Her unsuccessful 1975 campaign for a parliamentary seat from Châtellerault, a conservative city southwest of Paris, earned her the nickname *la battante* (the fighter). Cresson's combative campaign style began to pay off when she was elected mayor of Thure in 1977. Two years later she earned a seat in the European Parliament, but it was not until 1983 that Cresson led her most successful campaign and became mayor of Châtellerault. The only Socialist candidate in the municipal elections of that year to unseat a conservative mayor, Cresson held the position until her appointment as prime minister.

Cresson was appointed to her first cabinet-level position in 1981 when Mitterand named her minister of agriculture. Controversy followed Cresson's appointment to her first national office as farmers refused to follow her policies. Cresson blamed the stormy relationship on the conservative politics and sexism of the farmers. This would not be Cresson's last battle with sexism in French politics, but her tenure at the Ministry of Agricultural was successful. In spite of the farmers' dislike of her, their profits rose 10 percent in 1982.

In 1983 Cresson moved to the Ministry of Foreign Trade and Tourism, and in 1984 she added industrial redeployment to her portfolio. Her appointment to these positions coincided with the growing public sentiment against the nationalization of industry, or placing industry under government control. Cresson showed a willingness to compromise, however, when she diverged from staunch Socialist policies, which advocate no private ownership of property or business. Cresson took a hard-line approach, though, when it came to protecting the French economy from Japanese imports. Upon being placed in charge of foreign trade she began riding French scooters to demonstrate their superiority to Japanese counterparts as well as sending French executives abroad to promote French products.

Resigns as foreign minister

After being named minister of European affairs in 1988 Cresson continued her attacks on Japan and her policies that protected French-made goods. She regarded Japanese investments as aiming to conquer the world and destroy jobs, an opinion that she voiced when the Japanese prime minister visited Paris in January 1990. Cresson's sense of Japan as an invading enemy even began to carry racist overtones. Her anti-Japanese sentiment conflicted with the beliefs of then prime minister Michel Rocard, which resulted in Cresson's resignation as minister of European affairs in October 1990. She claimed that Rocard lacked an adequate industrial policy to deal with the current international economic situation, which would eventually lead to the weakening of France due to "insufficient mobilization."

Becomes prime minister

Cresson received the opportunity to correct the mistakes she saw in Rocard's policies when she replaced him as prime

minister in May 1991. She promised to be more careful than Rocard in giving money to industry, and she would demand results before giving more aid. But time showed Cresson's economic protectionism to be directed mainly toward Japan, which drew much attention from international observers. Despite fears of Japanese cultural and economic invasion, Cresson allowed the French computer company Groupe Bull to resume relations with NEC Corporation of Japan in June 1991. Cresson's Japan-bashing elicited strong criticism of her appointment as prime minister. Members of the Gaulist party (the strongest opposition to the Socialist party) as well as her own party had a hard time accepting her attacks on Japan.

Mitterand expected Cresson to introduce new social programs to stimulate growth, such as financial aid for education and job retraining. The political makeup of a small Communist representation in Parliament, however, made it difficult for Cresson to get support for the bills she believed necessary for social reform. She also became the target of satire when the

Edith Cresson with French President Francois Mitterrand in May 1991.

Bebete Show, a popular daily television program featuring satirical puppets, introduced a new character based on Cresson. She called the satire the same type of sexist hatred that she experienced while with the agricultural ministry. Cresson then made it her goal to fight against sexism in French politics. However, public rejection of this campaign, along with a decline in support of the Socialist party and her inability to pass bills, led to Cresson's downfall. She resigned on April 2, 1992, after less than a year in office.

Where to learn more

Bell, David S., Douglas Johnson, and Peter Morris, editors, *Biographical Dictionary of French Political Leaders since 1870,* Harvester Wheatsheaf, 1990.

Business Week, May 27, 1991.

New Republic, August 12, 1991.

Newsweek, May 27, 1991; July 1, 1991; July 22, 1991.

New York Times, May 16, 1991.

U.S. News & World Report, May 27, 1991.

Wall Street Journal, June 13, 1991.

Marie Curie

Born November 7, 1867
Warsaw, Poland
Died July 4, 1934
French Alps

Polish physicist and radiation chemist

Discovered polonium and radiation;
pioneered the use of X-rays;
won two Nobel Prizes

Marie Curie was the first woman to win a Nobel Prize, and one of the few scientists ever to win that award twice. In collaboration with her physicist husband, Pierre Curie, she developed and introduced the concept of radioactivity to the world. Working in primitive laboratory conditions, Curie investigated the nature of high-energy rays spontaneously produced by certain elements, and isolated two new radioactive elements, polonium and radium. Her scientific efforts also included the application of X-rays and radioactivity to medical treatments.

Christened Maria Sklodowska, Curie was born on November 7, 1867, in Warsaw, Poland. She was the fourth daughter and fifth child of schoolteachers whose ancestors had been wealthy landowners. Curie's parents considered learning to be important, so they encouraged their children's curiosity and creativity in a loving environment. The family's happiness was dimmed, however, when Curie was only five years old. Her mother, Bronislawa, contracted tuberculosis (a communi-

"All my mind was centered on my studies. All that I saw and learned that was new delighted me. It was like a new world opened to me, the world of science, which I was at last permitted to know in liberty."

cable disease primarily affecting the lungs) and had to avoid kissing or even touching her children. By the time Curie was 11, both her mother and her eldest sister, Zosia, had died. When she completed her elementary schooling, she entered Warsaw's "Floating University," an underground, revolutionary school that prepared young Polish students to become teachers.

Helps with sister's education

Curie left Warsaw at the age of 17, not for her own sake but for that of her older sister Bronya. Because Polish law prohibited higher education for women, both sisters wanted to go to school abroad. The family could not afford to send either of them, so Marie took a job as a governess to fund her sister's medical education in Paris. At first she accepted a post near her home in Warsaw, then she went to work for the Zorawskis, a family who lived some distance from Warsaw. Curie supplemented her formal teaching duties there by organizing a free school for the local peasant children. Casimir Zorawski, the family's eldest son, eventually fell in love with Curie and she agreed to marry him, but his parents objected vehemently. Marie was a fine governess, they argued, but Casimir should marry a much richer woman. Stunned by her employers' rejection, Curie finished her term with the Zorawskis and sought another position. She had spent a year in a third governess job before her sister Bronya finished medical school and summoned her to Paris.

Enrolls at the Sorbonne

In 1891, at the age of 24, Curie enrolled at the Sorbonne, becoming one of the few women in attendance at the Parisian university. Although Bronya and her family back home were helping Curie pay for her studies, living in Paris was quite expensive. Too proud to ask for help, she lived on a diet of buttered bread and tea and sometimes fruit or an egg. Since her room often had no heat, she stayed at the library as long as possible in order to stay warm and sometimes slept with all of her clothes piled on her bed. Becoming anemic, Curie fainted during class on at least one occasion. Nevertheless, in 1893 Curie received a degree in physics, finishing first in her class. The following year she earned a master's degree, this time graduating second in her class.

Marries Pierre Curie

Marie met Pierre Curie in 1894. They became friends and eventually married. Pierre accepted a job in Paris at the School of Industrial Physics and Chemistry (EPCI). Given lab space at the school, Marie spent eight hours a day on her investigations into the magnetic qualities of steel until she became pregnant with her first child, Irène, who was born in 1897. She then began work in earnest on her doctorate. Like many scientists, she was fascinated by French physicist Antoine-Henri Becquerel's discovery that the element uranium emitted rays that contained vast amounts of energy. Using the piezoelectric quartz electrometer developed by Pierre and his brother Jacques, Curie tested all the known elements to see if any of them, like uranium, caused the nearby air to conduct electricity. In the first year of her research, Curie coined the term *radioactivity* to describe this mysterious force. She later concluded that only thorium and uranium and their compounds were radioactive.

Conducts pioneering research

While other scientists had also investigated the radioactive characteristics of uranium and thorium, Curie noted that the minerals pitchblende and chalcolite released more rays than could be accounted for by either thorium or uranium. Curie

concluded that some other radioactive element must be causing the greater radioactivity. In July 1898 she and Pierre successfully extracted an element from pitchblende that was even more radioactive than uranium; they called it polonium in honor of Marie's homeland. Six months later the Curies discovered another radioactive substance embedded in the pitchblende.

Although the Curies had speculated that these elements existed, to prove their existence they still needed to describe them fully and calculate their atomic weight. In order to do so, Curie needed an abundant supply of pitchblende and a better laboratory. She arranged to get hundreds of kilograms of waste scraps from a pitchblende mining firm in her native Poland, and Pierre's EPCI supervisor offered the couple the use of a laboratory space. They worked together, with Marie performing the physically demanding job of chemically separating the pitchblende and Pierre analyzing the physical properties of the substances that Marie's separations produced. In

1902 the Curies announced that they had succeeded in preparing a decigram, or one-tenth of a gram, of pure radium chloride and had made an initial determination of radium's atomic weight. They had proven that radium is a separate chemical element. Marie took a position as a lecturer in physics at the Ecole Normal Superieure, becoming the first woman to teach there. In 1903 Curie became the first woman in France to complete her doctorate, graduating with highest honors.

Receives her first Nobel Prize

After Curie earned her doctorate, she and her husband began to achieve international recognition for their research. In November the couple received England's prestigious Humphry Davy Medal. The following month, along with Becquerel, they received the Nobel Prize in physics for their efforts in expanding scientific knowledge about radioactivity. Although Curie was the first woman ever to receive the prize, she and Pierre declined to attend the award ceremonies, pleading they were too tired to travel to Stockholm (they were suffering from an illness that would become known as radiation sickness). In December 1904 Marie gave birth to another daughter, Eve Denise. Despite the fact that both Pierre and Marie frequently suffered adverse effects from the radioactive materials with which they were in constant contact, their baby was born healthy. The Curies continued their work, occasionally taking vacations in the French countryside with their children. They had just returned from a vacation when, on April 19, 1906, tragedy struck. While walking in the congested Paris street traffic, Pierre was run over and killed by a heavy wagon.

A month after the accident, the University of Paris invited Curie to take over her husband's teaching position. She became the first woman ever to receive a post in higher education in France, although she was not named to a full professorship for two more years. During her work at the university she coined the terms *disintegration* and *transmutation.* In 1910, with her assistant Andre Debierne, Curie finally isolated pure radium metal and later wrote a description of uranium that could be used by scientists throughout the world.

Irène Joliot-Curie

In 1926 Irène Curie (1897-1956) married Frédéric Joliot (1900-1958), an assistant at the Radium Institute, where she became director two years before her mother's death. Together the Joliot-Curies (Frédéric changed his name after their marriage) continued the work of Marie and Pierre Curie on radioactivity. They shared the Nobel Prize in chemistry in 1935 for their study of artificial production of radioactive substances and in 1945 they helped start the French Atomic Energy Commission. Because of their membership in the French Communist Party, they were forced to resign from the commission in the early 1950s.

Wins second Nobel Prize

Curie was awarded the Nobel Prize again in 1911, this time for the discovery of the elements radium and polonium. She was the first scientist to win the Nobel twice. During World War I, she volunteered at the National Aid Society, then brought her expertise to the war front, instructing medical personnel in the practical applications of radiology. By the 1920s Curie was an international figure, although her health was failing and she was troubled by fatigue and cataracts. Despite her discomfort, Curie made a highly publicized tour of the United States in 1921. That same year the University of Paris completed the Institut Radium, or Radium Institute, enabling Curie to study radioactivity with a physician who could do research on radium therapy (the use of radium to treat disease).

Throughout the decade Curie continued her work in the laboratory, joined by her daughter, Irène Joliot-Curie, who was pursuing a doctorate. Because Curie's health continued to fail she was forced to spend more time away from the laboratory. As the result of prolonged exposure to radium, she contracted leukemia and died on July 4, 1934, in a nursing home in the French Alps. She was buried next to Pierre Curie in

Sceaux, France. In 1937 Eve Curie published a biography of her mother, *Madame Curie: A Biography by Eve Curie,* which has been translated into English.

Where to learn more

Birch, Beverly, *Marie Curie,* Gareth Stevens Publish-ing, 1988.

Parker, Steve, *Marie Curie and Radium,* HarperCollins, 1992.

Pflaum, Rosalynd, *Grand Obsession: Madame Curie and Her World,* Doubleday, 1989.

Pflaum, Rosalynd, *Marie Curie and Her Daughter Irène,* Lerner Publications, 1993.

Poynter, Margaret, *Marie Curie: Discoverer of Uranium,* Enslow Publishers, 1994.

Index

Boldface indicates main entries, italicized indicates volume numbers, and illustrations are marked by (ill.).

American Ballet Theatre *1:*26; *4:*929
American Book Award *4:*965
American Civil Liberties Union (ACLU) *2:*414
American Document *2:*440
American Exemplar Medal *1:*140
American Music Award *2:*329
American Negro Theater *2:*287
Amnesty International *1:*83
ANC (see African National Congress)
And a Voice to Sing With *1:*84
Anderson, Marian *1:***30-34,** 30 (ill.), 32 (ill.); *4:*840, 842, 995
Angelou, Maya *1:***35-39,** 35 (ill.), 38 (ill.); *2:*289
Anne Frank Foundation *2:*380
Annie Allen *1:*165
Anti-Semitism *1:*158; *3:*688-689; *4:*885
Apgar, Virginia *1:***40-43**
Apgar score *1:*40
Apollo *3:*544-545
Appalachian Spring *2:*440
April Twilights *1:*198
Aquino, Corazon *1:***44-49,** 44 (ill.), 48 (ill.) 133
Arden, Elizabeth *1:***50-53,** 50 (ill.), 53 (ill.)
Ashwari, Hanan *1:***54-58,** 54 (ill.), 57 (ill.)
Association of Artists for Freedom *2:*289
Astorga, Nora *1:***59-62,** 59 (ill.)
Atom bomb *2:*424; *4:*830
Atomic fission bomb *2:*422
Audubon Medal *1:*194
Auerbach, Charlotte *1:***63-66**
Aung San Suu Kyi *1:***67-71,** 67 (ill.), 70 (ill.)
Aunt Harriet's Underground Railroad in the Sky *4:*852
Azidothymidine (AZT) *2:*317, 321, 419-420

B

Babbitt, Natalie *1:***72-75,** 72 (ill.); *3:*768

Baca, Judith *1:***76- 79,** 76 (ill.)
Baez, Joan *1:***80-84,** 80 (ill.), 82 (ill.)
Baiul, Oksana *1:***85-90,** 85 (ill.), 88 (ill.)
Baker, Ella *1:***91-95,** 94 (ill.); *2:*450
Baker, Josephine *1:***96-101,** 96 (ill.), 100 (ill.)
Baker, Sara Josephine *1:***102-105,** 102 (ill.)
Balfour Agreement *1:*55
Balinese Character: A Photographic Analysis *3:*684
Ballet Alicia Alonso *1:*26-27
Ballet Nacional de Cuba *1:*25, 28-29
Ballet Russe de Monte Carlo *1:*27; *4:*927, 929
Baptism of Desire *2:*324
Barnett, Samuel *1:*11
Bates, Daisy *1:***106-110,** 106 (ill.), 109 (ill.), 166
Batista, Fulgencio *1:*27; *2:*327
Battle, Kathleen *1:*33, **111-115,** 111 (ill.), 113 (ill.)
Beauvoir, Simone de *1:***116-120,** 116 (ill.), 118 (ill.)
Beckonings *1:*167
Bedtime Stories *3:*651
The Beet Queen *2:*325
The Beginning Place *3:*614
Bell Burnell, Jocelyn *1:***121-124**
Beloved *3:*715, 717
Bessie Smith: 1925-1933 *4:*910
Bethune, Mary McLeod *1:***125-129,** 125 (ill.), 128 (ill.)
Bhutto, Benazir *1:***130-134,** 130 (ill.), 133 (ill.)
The Big Broadcast of 1938 *2:*472
Billboard *2:*328
Bingo Palace *2:*322
The Black Book *3:*717
Black Hearts in Battersea *1:*16
Black, Shirley Temple *1:***135-140,** 135 (ill.), 137 (ill.)
Blackburn, Elizabeth H. *1:***141-143**
Blair, Bonnie *1:***144-147,** 144 (ill.), 146 (ill.); *4:*995

Z